T0354484

44

DEGREES

Unveiling the Mystery
and
Magnitude of the Seasons of Joseph

KEVIN MCCOY HUNT

WESTBOW°
PRESS
A DIVISION OF THOMAS NELSON
& ZONDERVAN

Copyright © 2014 Kevin McCoy Hunt.

All rights reserved. No part of this book may be used or reproduced by any means, graphic, electronic, or mechanical, including photocopying, recording, taping or by any information storage retrieval system without the written permission of the publisher except in the case of brief quotations embodied in critical articles and reviews.

WestBow Press books may be ordered through booksellers or by contacting:

WestBow Press
A Division of Thomas Nelson & Zondervan
1663 Liberty Drive
Bloomington, IN 47403
www.westbowpress.com
1 (866) 928-1240

Because of the dynamic nature of the Internet, any web addresses or links contained in this book may have changed since publication and may no longer be valid. The views expressed in this work are solely those of the author and do not necessarily reflect the views of the publisher, and the publisher hereby disclaims any responsibility for them.

Any people depicted in stock imagery provided by Thinkstock are models, and such images are being used for illustrative purposes only.
Certain stock imagery © Thinkstock.

ISBN: 978-1-4908-4158-8 (sc)
ISBN: 978-1-4908-4159-5 (hc)
ISBN: 978-1-4908-4160-1 (e)

Library of Congress Control Number: 2014911108

Printed in the United States of America.

WestBow Press rev. date: 08/18/2014

All praises to God Almighty for allowing our mother, Hattie Viola Merchant Hunt, to grace this life and lay a foundation of love for God and man that touched so many lives in a short amount of years. Emmett G., Ronald C., and I were so blessed to have her as such.

I acknowledge that her untimely death is connected to my endowment of knowledge to record the enlightenment of 44° in due season. My destiny was set into motion at that time.

> We know that God makes all things work together for the good of those who love Him and are chosen to be a part of His plan.
> —Romans 8:28 NLT

CONTENTS

INTRODUCTION

Have you ever noticed something for the first time that grabs your attention and personal interests, and then, strangely, you begin to see it or hear about it everywhere? It's as if the item or subject is purposefully placed in front of you (seemingly for your eyes only) when you'd never paid any attention to it before. For example, once my wife and I purchased a car, thinking it was unique in color and style because we had never before seen one like it on the road. As soon as we purchased it, we frequently saw others like it around our town. Then we began to see it everywhere, seemingly in multiples! Of course, at that point it was too late to take it back to the car dealership. Perhaps this phenomenon simply means we are more conscious of things that are of interest to us than those things in which we have no interest.

Reading the Holy Bible as a preteen, I enjoyed the book of Genesis, the first book in the Bible. Reading it several times as a young person, the life of Joseph of Egypt drew me in more than the rest of the stories. More than thirty-five years later, the story still resonates and creates excitement within me, even above so many of the other wonderful characters in the ancient manuscripts. First, Joseph was so young and beloved, yet his own brothers sold him into slavery. This sounds like the end of a tragedy, but Joseph was eventually appointed the most powerful man in all of Egypt. If one understands the greatness of Egypt alone at the height of its dynasties, that's enough to appreciate why Joseph's life was and still is so inspirational today.

Interestingly, just as in the car scenario described above, I have been hearing more and more about Joseph of late. During the last several years, the topic of Joseph keeps popping up out of nowhere.

In October 2005, I was in prayerful study, working on a mystery to which the good Lord was opening my mind. Like Monk the investigator or Andy Griffith in the *Matlock* TV series, I was keyed in, almost in a trancelike state, when suddenly I heard a voice stating, "These are the seasons of Joseph." Ever since then, my heart and mind have heard and seen things I would have never paid any attention to before. Since then I have heard more and more about Joseph of Egypt.

A couple of years ago, I was helping a close family friend who was going through a rough time. Unexpectedly she said, "It seems like I keep hearing about Joseph a lot lately. What does it mean, Pastor?"

Another time several months later, I was coming home from church one Sunday afternoon when I received a phone call from my wife asking if I could stop at the grocery store and pick up a few needed items before coming home. When heading into the store, I saw a blast-from-the-past childhood friend who has flourished in ministry. I had not spoken to him in a while, since his older brother's funeral. He shared his renewed joy in his ministerial transition, and I was drawn into what he was saying. I was so glad to see him, and I sensed this was another meant-to-be encounter. Without preamble my friend shared with me the excitement he'd experienced in teaching people about the life of Joseph. My mind locked on the name. *Joseph!* My friend could have said Abraham or Moses or King David or Paul or the Virgin Mary's husband, Joseph, or the one and only Christ Jesus. But no, he was talking about Joseph of Egypt.

One day shortly thereafter when I went into my home office to get my reading glasses, a television commercial came on about visiting the Sight-n-Sound Theater in Lancaster, Pennsylvania. The area is known for its Amish population and their pre-nineteenth-century way of living. It is one of the most-visited theaters in Pennsylvania because of its theatrical renditions of different stories of the Bible. Playing at the Sight-n-Sound Millennium Theater was the story of Joseph of Egypt, and the commercial referenced the beauty and majesty of the performance. Of course I was interested in seeing the play! We had been to Sight-n-Sound a number of times, but this play had never been offered. I realized that once again this was one of the *seasons of Joseph effects* that was revealed to me back in 2005.

What is it about Joseph's life that has been getting so much fresh attention, whether in cartoons, movies, or Broadway theater shows? It is no longer just religious folks who are going over their Sunday school teachings or studying their Torah (the first 5 books of Moses in the Bible) lessons who speak about this giant of a man. Why isn't the life of King David, the apple of God's eye, discussed more often instead? King David is often referred to in the Scriptures, and rightfully so. The Scriptures in the Old Testament predicted that the Messiah of the ages to come is called the Son of David. In fact, his son, Solomon, was not only considered the wisest king of all time but also one of the most celebrated for his wealth and prestige. Yet none of those prestigious men receives the volume of affection and admiration that Joseph, the eleventh son of Jacob, receives. Why is that?

Recently the world stopped to memorialize the life and legacy of South Africa's Nelson Mandela, who lived his life to overcome the injustices of apartheid in his homeland, even after suffering imprisonment for twenty-seven years. His life touched many nations and international leaders. Nelson Mandela rose from imprisonment in 1990 to become his nation's first black president only four years later. Former US President Bill Clinton reiterated how Mandela chose to love and respect his political opposition, even placing those individuals in key roles in his cabinetry as president.

Other political leaders offered their reflections of this great man, whose life mimics that of Joseph, as he was also imprisoned and then worked to overcome his country's oppression and eventually rule that same country.

Former President George H. W. Bush stated, "As President, I watched in wonder how Nelson Mandela had the remarkable capacity to forgive his jailers … setting a powerful example of redemption and grace for us all."

- Britain's Prime Minister David Cameron reflected, "Tonight, one of the brightest lights of our world has gone out … Nelson Mandela was not just a hero of our time, but a hero of all time."
- Former President George W. Bush offered these words, "President Mandela was one of the great forces for freedom and equality of our time."
- Current U.S. President Barack Obama stated, "Through his fierce dignity and unbending will to sacrifice his own freedom for the freedom of others, Mandela transformed South Africa and moved all of us. His journey from a prisoner to a president embodied the promise that human beings and countries can change for the better."
- Muhammad Ali added, "His was a spirit born free, destined to soar above the rainbows. Today his spirit is soaring above the heavens. He is now free forever." [1]

Like Joseph, Nelson Mandela embodied and inherited much reverence from others. Even in his early days as a Bible student and teacher (at the end of his life, he acknowledged the Methodist faith), I am sure he read about the life of Joseph and the life of Moses and was filled with the wonder of a greater day of freedom for his people. If you listen and watch religious leaders around the country, Catholics, Protestants, and Muslims equally remain intrigued by the life of Joseph, who lived almost 3,800 years ago. His story touches the lifeline of human hope in the midst of the travesty of betrayal, which may be one of the hardest blows to overcome in life.

In the midst of Joseph's betrayal, he was exalted in an otherwise hostile nation that had looked down on Jews for being nomadic shepherds. Beyond Joseph's exaltation in Egypt, he helped save many

---

[1]   http://www.bbc.co.uk/news/uk-politics-25248490.

lives of those who were suffering from a severe famine around the known world.

As preachers and teachers, I believe we are attracted to Joseph because, no matter what he went through, the favor of *God changed the forecast of extreme sadness to rivers of gladness* on his behalf. What great hope to all who have experienced such heartache!

In the face of the unstable economic climate in the United States and abroad where unemployment remains high and the cost of living continues to creep upward, the story of Joseph encourages the downcast. *Better days are ahead!* The Joseph saga is not only about hope, but it also holds powerful principles to help us overcome the worst of times and enjoy the best of times with a sober mind. Even in the face of racial, religious, economic, and other social injustices, his story remains an example of not allowing negative opposition or adversities to have full control of one's destiny of a better life.

We can say that, other than Jesus, Abraham, and Moses, no one else holds the volume of influence like Joseph of Egypt. This influence goes far beyond him being a favored child of Jacob because of his attractiveness.

In this book we will look into qualitative reasoning as well as the prophecies that were spoken about Joseph, which may have been overlooked in previous teachings. I will also utilize the teaching of *gematria*, a sage Jewish methodology in which each letter of the alphabet carries a numerical value, and the calculation of the numerical equivalence of letters, words, or phrases helps us gain insight into links between otherwise-different concepts and explore the relationship of words and ideas.[2]

Just as numbers can be utilized to resolve measurements, volumes, and sizes, gematria works to help us understand the relationship of numbers and words in a Hebrew text. With any law, there is the *actual law*; how the law works and the process of how the law should be carried out. I will refer to gematria not in its fullness, but I will use the principle (how it works), as well as deductions based on

---

[2] http://www.inner.org/gematria/gematria.htm.

gematria throughout this book. Learning how gematria works within the subject of the season of Joseph will help us appreciate greater meaning and understanding throughout the text. What you read will become more alive and insightful.

During the course of this book, I will call my usage of gematria, *the principle, or spirit, of gematria.* It will help us to see deeper into the mind of God—the Designer of all things—who created all things with relation to purpose and destiny. Through the use of gematria, we will see that Joseph's life is *right now* on full course to touch the fabric of today's environment.

In Steve Greison's DVD documentary *The Search for the Real Mt. Sinai* (2003), Reverend Bob Grant, doctor of theology, says, "Tradition is a powerful thing ... and once you start fooling with tradition, even if it is legitimate evidence; it is very, very difficult for people to let go of that."

In this book, we will explore both tradition and legitimate evidence, using gematria. I ask that you keep an open mind during this exploration, and let God lead you, as He has led me, to a new level of understanding.

According to 1 Corinthians 13:13: "Three things will last forever; faith, hope, and love—and the greatest of these is love" (NLT). All of these things are powerfully grafted into the life of Joseph.

So I invite you, readers, both religious and nonreligious, to consider—and yes, *even enjoy!*—the intriguing knowledge that is about to be shared in this book and the aura that surrounds Joseph's amazing life. Be open-minded; consider new insights and perspectives into the holy Scriptures, and realize how they can translate into a greater dimension than how they may have been previously understood.

My goal in writing this book was, first, to obey the Lord God, who is the revealer of the secrets of men and the mysteries held within the book and to communicate these mysteries to you. Second, in the midst of the hopelessness and despair in today's society, I wish to provide a greater light of faith, hope, and love to a world that is being shaken on every side.

—Reverend Kevin McCoy Hunt

CHAPTER 1

DESTINY: MAJESTIC OR MYTHICAL?

The word *destiny* refers to a predetermined course of human and natural events. It is a concept that suggests there is a guiding force, or hand, providing direction in human or cosmic events, but the confines of human reasoning subjects the topic to many considerations. Many may consider destiny to be coincidental, while others believe it is inevitable and unchangeable. For most, destiny is connected to a Superior Being and/or Creator of the universe. My reason for discussing such a compelling topic here is not to debate its function but to declare that it does exist.

I believe in destiny but not in the sense that no matter what choices or decisions a person makes, they will not impact that person's future. I believe there are certain indefinable occurrences and events that work under a greater scenario and under the direction of a Sovereign Being (the Creator of the universe). I believe His will for mankind is for us to eventually become whole and at peace, which was the original design before disobedience came into the picture.

According to the written texts of the Major and Minor Prophets and other holy men, the Creator, through His mediating Savior called the *Messiah*, will eventually turn things around and create an oasis of love and peace on earth. There is also a predicted end for those who

1

choose evil over good, unrighteousness compared to right living. There are logic and principles that remain intact when determining your destiny; you will get out of it what you put into it. In other words, what you do, what you say, and what you think in your heart will place you on the right or wrong side of your intended destiny.

Jesus of Nazareth made a profound statement when He said, "And if a blind man guides a blind man, both will fall into a pit" (Matt. 15:14b NASB). In other words, what you believe, what you actually do, and what you say out of your mouth will impact the destiny that is before you.

Albert Einstein, arguably one of the greatest minds ever, understood the depths of science. Although he was not a very devout man, and neither did he study his own Jewish heritage from the Torah, he understood that it was reasonable for someone to believe in a more superior mind—one who has all knowledge of the universe. Einstein stated, "Strange is our situation here upon the Earth. Each of us comes for a short visit, not knowing why, yet sometimes seeming to a divine purpose."[3]

I must admit here that science is not my cup of tea, but I do believe one cannot explore destiny without truly considering the Greater Mind of intelligence in this vast, highly complex world. Einstein understood there was an interweaving of what the Highest Mind (our Creator) allowed and what Einstein controlled in his moral existence on earth. This intermingling of *what is* and *what is meant to be* is associated with His highest good and permits for allowances within the human culture. That highest good need not to be ignored. God willing, I will make reference to this great mind of thoughts and considerations at another time.

Even nonreligious people seem to believe in destiny, to some degree, especially when the phrase, "It was meant to be" is used. Can destiny be understood ahead of time? Can one's destiny be destroyed

---

3 "Einstein Quotes." *Albert Einstein*. GreenLight, LLC of The Hebrew University of Jerusalem, n.d. Web. 06 Jan. 2014. "My Credo," 1932. AEA 28-218

because of poor preparation, wrong choices, and improper work ethic? I believe in all the above. Then the question becomes: *Does destiny only come around in big equations? Or do the small, seemingly less important incidents matter?* I believe destiny affects all arenas, as big things are made up of the smaller things. For instance, we might consider the destiny of nations and their challenges, but we can also look at the sports and entertainment world.

I remember when the Major League Baseball team, the Philadelphia Phillies, finally won the National League Eastern Title in 2008 by beating the Los Angeles Dodgers. The Philly Sports Talk Radio personality, Angelo Cataldi, admitted that he was a believer in destiny but was not necessarily a religiously devout person. His morning show included conversations about the Fightin' Phils as they won round by round, until they finally won the World Series. Was it destiny for the Phillies to win it all?

After all, it was believed that a Philadelphia sports franchise could not win a major championship, and indeed they had lost for over twenty years, purportedly because of the "Curse of Billy Penn."[4] This so-called curse was said to have started when the buildings being constructed in the city of Philadelphia were being built taller than the William "Billy" Penn statue located in central Philly. When one of the largest cable companies in the United States, Comcast, decided to place a small statue of William Penn on its tallest building in the metropolitan area in 2007, one year later the Philadelphia Phillies had a banner season.

In the weeks leading up to winning the World Series, I remember hearing heartfelt testimonials of people calling into the sports talk show, wishing that their deceased loved ones could be there to witness what was possibly going to take place in the World Series. Many of the callers were convinced that it was *written in the heavens* for the Phillies to finally win it all. Well, what do you expect from fans so

---

[4] http://corporate.comcast.com/comcast-voices/comcast-and-the-curse-of-billy-penn.

passionate about the Phillies? If you watched the series, you know that the Phillies played well enough to stay a measure ahead in each game to secure a win. They did not stomp on anyone, but they always did just enough, and the ball always seemed to bounce their way.

During game 5 of the final series, the umpires stopped play in the middle of the game, delaying for two days because of the cold and rainy inclement weather.[5] I've never seen anything like it, and national sports commentators agreed. When they resumed the game and the final pitch was made, the Tampa Bay Rays' batter struck out. The Phillies won the game and became the 2008 World Series Champions. For Phillies fans, of which I am one, it was a great feeling. But was it destiny? Can destiny and favoritism from the heavens be in sync with earthly events for personal recreation as well as other important matters of life?

The Phillies' relief pitcher in that final game was the right-handed closer, Brad Lidge. Wearing the number 54, he made the final out by striking out a left-handed batter. Ironically, twenty-five years earlier in1983, the Phillies had just the opposite scenario happen to them when winning the World Series. It was a left-handed reliever named Tug McGraw, who wore the number 45, who struck out a right-handed batter to win the game. This juxtaposition of facts is uncanny.

Could someone be looking down from the heavens upon such a momentous event? It is interesting that the mother of Phillies manager, Charlie Manuel, had just passed away right before one of the earlier National League Championship games. Charlie interviewed and shared that his mother told him just before she died that the team was going to win it all.[6] What makes me think twice about the circumstances of the Phillies team as being a part of destiny is that on the same day Charlie's mother passed, the starting centerfielder Shane Victorino's grandmother died too. Is it a coincidence that they died on the same day? The Phillies won that series and eventually the World Series.

---

[5] http://articles.latimes.com/2008/oct/11/sports/sp-nlside11.

[6] http://mlb.mlb.com/mlb/news/postseason/traces.jsp?loc=traces_manuel.

I believe in providential destiny because I believe wholeheartedly in the divine power of a Creator who makes all things possible and who knows all things ahead of time. This is called *omniscience*. He moves things and allows things to occur for redemptive and judgmental reasons beyond our understanding at times. Call it a feeling or a hunch, but I believe Charlie's mother spiritually sensed something, spoke it and it came to pass. After all, she was a very spiritual woman, and Charlie's father was a Pentecostal pastor before his early death. I believe this not only because I was raised up with a religious foundation but because I have many practical reasons and experiences that allow me to reflect on happenstance and affirm my intuition about things. If I reflect long enough on a situation, I can usually look back and see that the hand of God was in the midst of an event, though I might have overlooked it at first.

The following story is an illustration of my personal experiences with destiny. When I was in third grade at the Terry Elementary School of Coatesville, Pennsylvania, we had a wonderful teacher in Mrs. Josephine Stokes, who taught us about various cultures and customs around the world. She assigned a class project on the customs of the Orient, featuring the Japanese culture. In the spring of that year, our teacher showed us photographs and artwork of that particular culture and displayed some of the things we learned. A few of us were selected to work on a calendar with a Japanese-styled home on it. A classmate, Missy Brown, who is still my friend today, had good penmanship and took care of the basic calendar dates. She colored in our commencement date of May 5 in red marker on off-white cloth material. I primarily did the artwork for the Japanese-styled house. When our presentation day arrived, we ate rice from wooden bowls with Japanese chopsticks, we wore conical shaped hats, and some students even dressed in kimono robes.

At the end of the day during cleanup, our teacher wanted us to take everything home instead of keeping it on display in the classroom. I wanted my friend to take our project home, but she insisted I take it home. She and I went back and forth.

"You can take the calendar home," I would say.

"No, you can take the calendar home," she insisted.

Eventually her strong will won the tussle of kindness, and I ended up taking the calendar home. I placed it in the back of my closet full of piled-up stuff.

Two years later my family experienced a heart-wrenching loss. My mother, Hattie Merchant Hunt, passed away at the early age of forty-four from the devastating effects of chemo-radiation treatment while battling breast cancer. My father and his three sons' lives were dramatically affected, and our recovery from this devastation was slow. Through everything, my father never stopped taking us to church, and we never stopped being involved in the Union Baptist Church of South Coatesville, Pennsylvania.

After my mother's death, I dealt with weighty inner doubts. "Why Lord?" I asked. "If You are really there for Your people, then why, Lord, why?" I went through times of rebellion, as my father J. Emmett Hunt's quality time with me was very limited. He was a self-employed young proprietor of a funeral home business and was active in community affairs. He did the best he could in raising his three sons. To be honest, I briefly questioned whether God really existed.

My mom was as sweet as they come. Her parents, Mrs. Virginia and Mr. Golden Merchant, raised her. She was a faithful member of the Bethel A.M.E. Church of South Coatesville before marrying my father. She loved God and mankind, both white and black. That's pretty good for someone who grew up in a less-tolerant, culturally insensitive society. It was instilled in her, and she passed on this bit of wisdom to others: "You gotta love everybody if you wanna go to heaven." She would go to bed with a Bible on her chest, falling asleep after a full day of hard work at the Social Security office in West Chester, Pennsylvania.

During that trying time of my life, I strayed from God as I ran with some of the guys from my neighborhood, especially during the summertime. We were defiant boys, and I learned to cuss for the first time to try to fit in.

When I was in the seventh or eighth grade, as I was going through my closet looking for something, I came across the calendar from my third-grade project. It was rolled up like a scroll, and when I opened it to reminisce in good times, I was silenced and eventually became trance-like, staring at the date of our Japanese cultural day. The red-colored date, May 5, was the very day my mother passed.

I glared at the calendar, and with God as my witness, I heard an overwhelming phrase in my mind, as loudly and clearly as if it were spoken into my ear. "I already have your mother, and I will take care of you too."

It was a God moment for me. I became sad, thinking about my mother's death. I shed tears, yet I felt relieved on the inside, realizing the God I wanted to believe in had finally spoken clearly to my heart—and above all, He cared about me. I rolled up the calendar and put it back into the closet with renewed confidence that somehow God was going to look after me, along with my family and close acquaintances. I did not know it then, but I know now that it was all part of my destiny.

When I was growing up, we had on the wall two pictures of my parents' wedding from April 1950. One photo of the bride and groom was taken from the waist up, and the other was a full-length shot. Years later, when my father remarried in 1975, the pictures were taken down. Sadly, my father passed away in 1997, and he was buried next to my mother. My siblings and I never saw those pictures again.

Years later at my brother Emmett Golden Hunt's sixtieth birthday celebration, his wife, Arvilla, invited a lot of family and acquaintances, including a long-lost cousin from South Carolina, Shirley Blanding-Madison. My mother's parents originated from Monk's Corner, South Carolina before moving north to Coatesville, Pennsylvania. My mother and Shirley's grandmother were first cousins and the best of kin. Shirley gave Emmett G. a photograph of my parents' actual wedding party! That's right, the whole wedding party! The photo includes relatives who have all passed away, plus a young flower girl, who is none other than Diana Robinson Lewis, who was recently inducted into The Michigan State Journalist Hall of Fame. Now that's providential destiny.

Also attending the party was our only first cousin on both sides of the family, Danita (Dee Dee), and her oldest son, Shawn. Living outside of Washington, DC, area, Shawn decided to become a college student at South Carolina State in the mid-1990s, when a bizarre accident occurred. He was shot in the head, tragically causing him to permanently lose his sight in both eyes. Miraculously, his life was spared! Fortunately, our cousin Shawn has been an inspiration for everyone who meets him over the years. He graduated from the University of Maryland, earning bachelor's and master's degrees! He has a beautiful wife and enjoys a successful career working as a social work professional, in spite of any adversities.

After nearly forty years of separation, we discovered that Shirley, who brought up the wedding picture from South Carolina, just happened to be a professor at South Carolina State where the accident took place and was the person in charge of the department that works with the blind society through the school. Dee Dee and Shirley met for the first time at the celebration and introduced Shawn. And yes, Shawn and his wife were invited to go back down to the very school where it all happened. He was the keynote speaker of a special event for the blind, where his dad, Anthony, Sr. remarked, "He blew them away with his speech and experience!"

My cousin Shawn spoke to others who were dealing with the affliction of blindness and encouraged them beyond description. Sounds too ironic to be true, huh? Was this providence or what?

I'd like to share with you one last detail of the event: Shawn never knew that when he chose to attend college there, he was practically in the backyard of where his great-grandparents (the Merchants) grew up. He represented the fourth generation coming home. You will discover in later chapters why this fourth-generation detail is so powerful.

The Scriptures seem to reflect the greater plan of God on a consistent basis. For instance, in the word of the prophets, we often read, "And it came to pass ..." Something happens as the result of something else, also known as *cause and effect*. One thing leads to another until a major event unfolds to the exuberance of the people who were the subject of the prophecy; or a costly judgment occurs based upon actions of disobedience by the same people. The authors of the Scriptures, namely historical scribes and prophets, understood that the Maker and Creator had an intimate plan for mankind, and events were allowed and foreseen by His greatness. Furthermore, it was understood by the wisest man who ever lived, King Solomon, that life has repetitive cycles, from generation to generation. "Nothing is new under the sun" (Eccl.1:9 NIV).

I have many examples of destiny after living over fifty years now. During my last year at Terry Elementary School, there was a new kid in town, and we became good friends. When we were in sixth grade, he and his family moved out of state. I never forgot about him, as I thought he was a special person. I cannot fully recall knowing that he was a pastor's son or whether his father's job transferred him out of state, but I knew he belonged to the Church of Nazarene denomination, located up the street from our elementary school. After graduating from high school, I became a minister. For seven years I was groomed at my home church, and then I left and founded another local congregation. Within seven years, we purchased the very same building and parsonage where my friend's father led as a clergyman. Strange... huh? After many years of being in the property, I was finally able to contact my friend, and to my surprise and excitement, I learned he is now a pastor, too! Destiny? Maybe.

I could go on and on about divine intervention. These crossroads of extraordinary events have me fully convinced that a greater plan unfolds. Even when you look at American history and the lives of great men such as George Washington, Abraham Lincoln, Frederick Douglass, and Rev. Dr. Martin Luther King, Jr., and others, it is a testament that a greater hand in their lives connects them to their destinies.

9

Abraham Lincoln supposedly had a premonition of his death and saw himself laid out in his own casket before his fatal day.[7] Was his destiny and his life directed by a Greater One? I believe that's the case.

During the American Revolutionary War, a sharp-shooting Indian warrior made reference that he shot seventeen flares at General George Washington without hitting the man in battle. A lady named Mary Draper, who was captured at the time, overheard a conversation between the Indians and some French soldiers.[8] They shared how an Indian chief named Red Hawk told them that he shot Washington eleven times without killing him. His conclusion was that the Great Spirit was simply protecting him.[9] Was destiny at hand, overcoming the present distress of the time? I think so.

While General Washington and his troops were immensely suffering through the winter of 1777 in Valley Forge, Pennsylvania, our eventual first president had a vision that came to pass, and this has been related and preserved in the US Archives in Washington, DC. The vision, as accounted by Anthony Sherman, stated that a female angelic presence visited Washington, and referred to him over and over again as the "Son of the Republic."[10] The vision provided prophetic scenarios that concluded a nation would be birthed and would overcome several warlike challenges in the years ahead, including winning the American Revolutionary War. It has been interpreted that the second battle described seems to have been the War of 1812.[11] This vision apparently gave Washington greater hope and faith that the providence of heaven was not only with him, but also over the future of the United States of America.

Growing up, I learned that of the fifty-six signatories of the Declaration of Independence, only two eventually became president of the United States: John Adams and Thomas Jefferson. Though the

---

[7] Stone, 2001.
[8] Ibid.
[9] Ibid.
[10] Ibid.
[11] Ibid.

declaration was signed on July 2, it was not approved by Congress until July 4; hence, July 4 is considered Independence Day in the United States. What is so unusual is that both Adams and Jefferson died on July 4, 1826! Not the forty-sixth, forty-eighth, or fifty-second year, but the fiftieth year after the approval of the Declaration of Independence.

The number 50 is an important number globally. Particularly in my culture, the number 50 is held in high esteem. Someone turning fifty years old—a half century—is a big deal. One's fiftieth birthday or fiftieth anniversary is a blessing. In my opinion, twenty-five years is great, but fifty is the magic number.

But why 50?

The number 50 in the Bible represents the year of jubilee and represents liberty—freedom from bondage. It comes from the book of Leviticus, the book of the Mosaic priesthood and ceremonial laws. Every forty-nine years, after seven sabbatical years (seven sets of seven years), the following year, the fiftieth, is considered a time of celebration and renewal, as all debts were eliminated from families, and all land was restored that was lost or loaned out. This was God's plan, through Moses, for the nation of Israel to remain a hopeful, prosperous community. This kept generations from remaining perpetually poor, and many of our debt laws to this day are influenced by this original thought.

If something goes against your credit rating, or your driving record, like a DUI, after seven years, the debt or offense, is removed. This law of mercy is why many formerly bankrupted institutions and businesses are prospering now. Chapter 11 and chapter 13 bankruptcies have been a saving grace for many people over the years. I am not referring to abuse of the system because abuse can occur anywhere liberty is instituted. But it is God's will to see all men come to liberty, and this law of 50 is one of the central principles of living as a civil humanity.

As a matter of fact, Leviticus 25:10, in part, is written on the Liberty Bell: "And you shall hallow [set aside as reverent] the fiftieth year and proclaim liberty throughout all the inhabitants thereof ..."

Considering these facts, were the simultaneous deaths of John Adams and Thomas Jefferson orchestrated by the Sovereign One? Again, I believe this is true. Their deaths seem to underline the significant reverence we need concerning the important essence of this country, the United States. Securing "liberty and justice for all" always needs to be in the forefront of the minds of all Americans as we work with and consider negotiations with foreign and allied nations. The price of liberty is high, and it should never, ever be taken for granted or abused without considering the divine blessing that supports that right. I believe it was destiny that these two men of greatness died on the same day in the same year, to further stamp the fact that the destiny of the United States was to bring its citizens and influence nations in the essence of liberty and justice for all. This true liberty is birthed by faith in its Creator.

In a C-SPAN documentary of the auction sale of *The Acts of Congress,* an annotated copy of George Washington's text, Ann Bookout was interviewed.[12,13] While waiting in the corridors of Christie's Auction House in New York, Mrs. Bookout was asked if she had received her bid paddle, and she replied, "No."

The man left and soon returned with a bid paddle, indicating *222* as her bid number.

Mrs. Bookout took comfort when she quickly realized that this number represented Washington's birthday: February 22, or 2/22. She stated that, in her heart, she knew it was going to be a good day for her to win the bid and purchase the precious document—the book Washington read prior to passing the Bill of Rights. Mrs. Bookout intended to return the book back to place where it began, to Mount Vernon, Virginia, where it now resides in the Washington National Library.

---

[12] "George Washington's Copy of the Constitution." *C-SPAN Video Library.* American History TV, 22 June 2012. Web. 18 Dec. 2013.

[13] "Post-Sale Release: George Washington's Acts of Congress." New York, 22 June 2012. Press Release. *Christie's,* 22 June 2012. Web. 18 Dec. 2012.

The book sold at auction for $9,826,500,[14] (gematria thirty, or three), and after 223 years (gematria seven), it came to rest in its original place.

Was this actually destiny or just general coincidences by mathematical hypothesis? Is there a greater plan, or do things just occur by happenstance?

Some of my favorite and unusual examples of destiny and repeated history are the parallels of Abraham Lincoln and John Fitzgerald Kennedy. These two were born and lived approximately one hundred years apart, yet their lives were *too much* in harmony not to consider divine or spiritual intervention of some sort. Listed here are but a few of the coordinating events in the lives of these two US presidents:

- Lincoln was elected in 1860, and Kennedy was elected in 1960—one hundred years apart.
- Both of their vice presidents were named Johnson: Andrew Johnson and Lyndon Johnson.
- Andrew Johnson was born in 1808, and Lyndon Johnson in 1908—one hundred years apart.
- John Wilkes Booth (Lincoln's assassin) was born in 1839, and Lee Harvey Oswald (Kennedy's accused assassin) was born in 1939.
- The names Lincoln and Kennedy each contain seven letters.
- The names John Wilkes Booth and Lee Harvey Oswald each contain fifteen letters.
- The names Andrew Johnson and Lyndon Johnson have thirteen letters each.
- Both vice presidents were southern Democratic senators before being elected.
- Both presidents had highly contested elections.
- Both were involved in violations and corrections regarding civil rights.

<hr/>

[14] http://www.christies.com/about/press-center/releases/pressrelease.aspx?pressreleaseid=5688

- Both presidents were US congressmen before becoming presidents.
- Both were fatally shot on a Friday.
- Both were shot in the head.
- Each man was shot in the presence of his wife.
- Both experienced the death of a child as presidents.
- Lincoln had a secretary named Kennedy, and Kennedy had a secretary named Lincoln.
- Each of secretaries warned the presidents not to go to the places where they were killed.
- Both assassins were killed before standing trial.
- Lincoln was shot in Ford's theater, and Kennedy was shot while in a Ford Lincoln limousine.

These comparisons are relatively well known, but nonetheless they remain astonishing. What is the meaning behind all of this? If the facts are true, does it seem more like a fictional story of created parallels? The principles and patterns of the comparisons are amazing. This phenomenon is actually an example of a hundred-year cycle of predestination. It is not simply that so much coincidence occurred, but it also depicts the beginning and the ending of a thing. Such an event draws a line in the sand. What was actually going on? What is the message behind this mysterious juxtaposition? Surely there is some kind of destiny involved. I will refer to this interwoven storyline in later chapters of this book to explain the divine nature of the occurrence.

This form of providential destiny was already in the works of the main character of this book, Joseph of Egypt. Joseph grew up under the tents of his father Jacob and their household. As a teenager Joseph dreamed strange dreams depicting him as being a ruler one day, one who ruled over his brothers and sister. His family found these dreams deplorable. After all, Joseph had ten brothers and one sister who were older than he was, and he was barely old enough to be allowed off the family property alone.

As referred to in the introduction, Joseph is a central figure of epic proportions. To the excitement and pleasure of many who have understood how valuable of a character Joseph was in the holy writings, I am just as glad to share with you a summary of his life and some prevailing characteristics of a life worthy of adoration. Albert Einstein is quoted as saying, "Try not to be a person of success, but rather a person of virtue ... a man of value."[15] Joseph possessed the best of both worlds as virtue and value introduced him to success. If there ever was a king-like person with the Midas touch, it was Joseph, hands down.

---

[15] "Einstein Quotes." *Albert Einstein.* GreenLight, LLC of The Hebrew University of Jerusalem, n.d. Web. 06 Jan. 2014. Quoted by William Miller in Life Magazine, May 2, 1955.

CHAPTER 2

A TREMENDOUS LIFE

R emember the wonderful old television series *Eight Is Enough,*
starring Dick Van Patten and Diana Hyland, along with Susan
Richardson from my hometown of Coatesville?[16] What about *Good
Times,* starring John Amos and Esther Rolle?[17] All of these shows
depicted family squabbles, the highs of family togetherness, the
lows of sibling rivalries and personal life fiascos. At times they were
simply dysfunctional, to say the least. I know something about this
by observing and hearing about my own family's stories; my father
was the fourth of twelve children born of James Claude and Roberta
Stith Hunt. Whether fictional favorites or reality TV, the more the
merrier is a stretch of the imagination. Then add to the equation that
of having the same father, but several mothers, all with children in
the same household? That is going to be an energized environment,
one way or another.

We will see that Joseph's family experienced this same kind of
large-family function and dysfunction beginning decades before
his birth. As wonderful as the life and greatness of Abraham was,
including the miraculous birth and life of his second son, Isaac, it

---

16 http://en.wikipedia.org/wiki/Eight_Is_Enough.
17 http://en.wikipedia.org/wiki/Good_Times.

wasn't until the life of Jacob, the youngest of Isaac's twins, that the nation eventually called Israel, which was promised to Abraham, started to grow. In Abraham's first one hundred forty years, he had only two children, Ishmael and Isaac. Isaac and his wife Rebekah had twin boys, Jacob and Esau. The nation of Israel and the many nations that would come from the lineage of Abraham were not off to a good start. When Jacob finally married, he was tricked into marrying two sisters, the daughters of Laban. Servant girls were given to both wives as marriage gifts. These servant girls eventually became concubines in the cultural arrangement of marriage. Both concubines bore children under Rachel and Leah. Leah, the oldest sister, had six sons, and her servant girl had two sons and one daughter, while Rachel had two sons, and her servant girl had two sons.

Many difficult and sometimes strange happenings took place during the twenty-year span of Jacob's stay at Laban's homestead. Jacob asked for the right to earn Rachel as his wife by working for Laban for seven years. Laban accordingly promised Jacob that he could have the hand of his daughter, Rachel. When seven years passed, Jacob followed the custom of the day, whereby the groom would stay in his tent, and his wife-to-be would come into the tent to sleep and consummate the marriage after arrangement by covenant agreement and a religious ceremony. Unfortunately, the following morning, Jacob discovered that Leah, Rachel's sister, had taken her place!

Jacob disputed the matter, but home-field advantage was already in play. Laban explained that it was customary for the oldest sister to marry before the younger sister. The intimacy between Jacob and Leah that took place officially united the two as husband and wife. Laban then reoffered his daughter Rachel to Jacob in exchange for another seven years of service. Jacob agreed. This story emphasized that Jacob loved Rachel so much that the first seven years went by quickly.

There are differences of opinion here, but I will share my thoughts about his uniting with Rachel. I believe he received Rachel immediately in the seven-year second agreement, and Laban allowed this because the man's word was his bond. Laban knew what he had in Jacob and believed he could trust him to fulfill his obligation.

A second reason I believe Jacob received Rachel right away is because of the amount of time it would take to have thirteen children. The story says that after twenty years of service, Jacob and his family left Laban with his family (Gen. 28–30).

More convincingly, I sense that Rachel became Jacob's wife immediately and not seven additional years later because the infighting for Jacob's affection and bearing children seemed to have started right after the marriages. The agreement to work seven more years was an agreement of credit. During the birth of Leah's children, there were already words and names of the children that spoke of Leah's desire to win Jacob's affection over his love for her sister. For all the children except for Benjamin to be born in the thirteen-year span (twenty years minus seven years), childbearing had to take place right after marriage.

For at least five years, Rachel was barren, and the decision was made to allow her servant girl, Bilhah, to have surrogate births, which produced two sons. After all, Leah had the first four sons in a row, so the competition between the sisters was on! But after sons Dan and Naphtali were born to Rachel's servant Bilhah, Leah decided to offer her servant girl to Jacob, as she was no longer bearing children. Leah's servant Zilpah birthed two more sons to Jacob. Zilpah also bore Jacob's first and only daughter, Dinah. Doesn't this story sound incredible? I tell people occasionally, "Why watch soap operas when you can read the Bible?"

After years of being barren, Rachel cried out to God in desperation, and the Lord heard her voice, allowing her to have her firstborn, Joseph. Jacob had Joseph at the age of ninety,[18] and Joseph became Jacob's most-heralded son. Jacob finally had a son with the woman he most adored, the woman who smote his heart from the beginning.

---

[18] http://www.biblecharts.org/oldtestament/interestingfactsaboutjoseph.pdf.

Sadly, the birth of her last child, Benjamin, cost Rachel her life, and she died during childbirth.

We understand, then, why Jacob favored Joseph the most. Joseph was born after a long period of waiting as the love of Jacob's life. But when there is this kind of affection in a triangular relationship with a competitive environment of envy and jealousy, watch out! It was this kind of atmosphere that produced the eventual arrangement that fulfilled what God had promised Abraham. Jacob's beloved son Joseph was not only a handsome young man, but he was also extremely gifted. It is amazing how some of the most gifted people who rose to a high level of success came from difficult circumstances that, many times, they had no control over.

By the age of seventeen, Joseph was reputed to be the snitch in the family. Of course, no one likes a snitch or a tattletale. Apparently Joseph notoriously informed his father and mother of the whereabouts of his brothers, and his brothers became aware of this. On top of that, Jacob gave Joseph a coat that distinguished him from the rest of his ten older brothers. It was described as a coat of many colors. No matter what Jacob's intent was in favoring his son with this vibrant gift, it proved to be an unwise decision, as this father did not seem to understand the depth of his older sons' negative feelings toward Joseph. Jacob's insensitivity created additional problems down the line, and in that particular powder-keg community, we can sense trouble brewing without actually being there.

The insensitivity of Jacob was also evident in his son, Joseph. When Joseph had a dream that he and his brothers were gathering and binding sheaves, his sheaves stood above the others, and in fact, their sheaves bowed before his, as subjects would bow before a king.

So what did Joseph do? Instead of consulting with his father, he went and told his brothers about his strange dream. The storyline has already led us to the fact that the brothers did not speak to Joseph with kindness because of his flamboyant coat and the perceived preferential treatment he received. Then Joseph added salt to the wound by telling them about the dream.

Joseph had his second predestination dream of the sun, moon, and stars, all bowing before him in the midst of a starry universe as indicated by this fine art work by Jeff Quick of Moodflow, called, "Before the Storm". The Creator used this backdrop to emphasize the eternal nature of the blessings that would one day come to pass in Joseph's life.

The King James Version of the Bible states, "They hated him yet the more" (Gen. 37:5). The word *hate* means "to abhor or despise with great passion."[19] Even with this kind of negative reaction, Joseph had another confirming dream, this one about the sun, moon and eleven stars, and in this dream they all bowed to him. Can you believe Joseph told his brothers and his father about the dream? Yes, he did! Jacob questioned Joseph's dream, unwilling to accept it, but he continued to ponder it in his heart, as he knew his son had a sixth sense.

Why would it be predestined for Joseph to rule over his own mother and father? This does not appear to be logical or even honorable in the sight of God concerning the proper morals of

---

[19] http://www.thefreedictionary.com/hate.

respect. Jacob believed the sun and moon represented him and his wife, Leah. After all, Rachel died giving birth to Jacob's twelfth and final son, Benjamin. Leah alone now carried the status of wife.

We again see Jacob's insensitivity as a father when he sends Joseph, the snitch and golden child, to find his brothers, who were several miles away shepherding the grazing sheep herds and other flocks. Envy of their brother now fully exploded in the brothers' hearts. Joseph's older brothers recognized him on his way to find them, and they plotted to kill him. The oldest, Reuben, talked the other brothers out of it, and they eventually decided to just put him into a pit while they decided what to do next. Later that day a caravan of nomadic traders came by, and Judah made the suggestion to sell Joseph to profit from the situation (Gen. 37). The brothers agreed on the plan and sold Joseph to the Midianite traders. We find out later in the story that Reuben was not there when this transaction took place.

Reuben found out what his brothers had done, and he tore his clothes in grief. He tried to figure out how to get Joseph back home safely to their father. Apparently his conscience finally kicked in, and he realized his brothers were set on not only hurting Joseph but also severely wounding their father, Jacob, for his blatant favoritism.

Next to the death of Rachel (approximately seven years earlier), Jacob learned the most horrific news—his beloved son Joseph had been presumably killed by a wild animal, and the only returning evidence was the blood-soaked coat of many colors. There was no other coat like that one, so it had to be Joseph's. Jacob was consumed with such unbearable grief that only the passage of time could renew his hopes again. The holy recording states that he could not be comforted (Gen. 37:35).

Joseph's brothers masterminded this charade of deception by killing one of the animals from the herd and dipping Joseph's coat in the blood. They did not kill him physically, but oh my, they killed him in spirit. They literally sold their brother into a land where, at the time, they had never traveled. Once the deal was done, it was as if Joseph was dead.

This wasn't the first time Jacob was involved in envy and deception. Jacob was a part of a heart-wrenching, conniving plot with his mother Rebekah when they tricked his nearly blinded father, Isaac, into giving Jacob the birthright and blessing customarily given to the firstborn son. Esau was the eldest son and should have been given this most sacred honor. This deceitful plot cost Esau the eventual headship of the nation of promise (Gen. 26:24 NLT). This event cost Jacob dearly, as this same spirit of trickery visited his envious sons. We will see later in the next chapter how his treacherous sons weighed in on the anguish of the soul years later.

After being sold to the Midianites, Joseph was carted off on a three-week journey to Egypt, where he was purchased by Potiphar, a captain of Pharaoh's guard in the slave trade (Gen. 39:1-2).

Joseph soon became noticeably successful at his tasks and was found to be trustworthy enough to manage all of Potiphar's servants and property. The story goes on to say that Joseph prospered in everything he did because the Lord was with him. The captain sensed this, and his whole household prospered as a result. Joseph was so efficient that Potiphar placed everything, including his personal goods, into Joseph's charge.

But soon a problem arose. Potiphar's wife began to lust for Joseph, and Joseph sought to avoid her, without informing his master. One day Potiphar's wife tried to force herself on Joseph, and he ran away, leaving behind his outer cloak. She then treacherously told her husband that Joseph had forced himself on her, and Potiphar threw Joseph in the king's prison. It was actually a miracle that Joseph was not put to death at that point. According to some interpretations, some believe Potiphar really was not convinced Joseph had actually committed this act. But because he was not only a slave but was a slave of a foreign culture, it would have been uncustomary for Potiphar to believe Joseph's word over his wife, thus hurting Potiphar's status as a high officer of Pharaoh.

However it happened, Potiphar still had a heart for Joseph and valued him too much to have him killed immediately. Providentially, this same aura was over Joseph when his brothers wanted to kill him. Perhaps like Reuben, Potiphar reconsidered how to save Joseph's life, or at least try to discern what actually happened. Potiphar may have known this tendency existed within his wife, and perhaps he knew deep inside that Joseph was not the initiator of any sexual harassment.

Joseph was thus thrown into Pharaoh's prison, where he was put to work. The prison master found Joseph to be so profitable in work ethic and administration that he promoted Joseph as the head of Pharaoh's prisoner system. This kind of favor was bestowed on Joseph, and nothing could be touched or handled in the prison without his permission. That is exactly the same scenario that occurred under Potiphar. Since Potiphar was in a greater position than the prison warden was, I wonder if perhaps the warden conferred with Potiphar about Joseph's past history. Everything prospered under Joseph's leadership because of his abundant favor.

In the meantime, the pharaoh was upset with two of his officers, the chief baker and chief butler, and had them thrown into prison. There they met Joseph, and Joseph noticed how greatly troubled they were. Both had experienced disturbing dreams that they could not interpret. Joseph asked them what was wrong, and the chief butler shared his vivid dream. Joseph interpreted the dream and shared with him the good news of how he would be released from prison and restored back to his position as chief butler in Pharaoh's court. Joseph was sure of his interpretation and asked the chief butler to please remember him before Pharaoh. The chief baker listened and asked Joseph to interpret his dream too. Joseph heard his dream, but unfortunately, it had a different interpretation. Joseph told the baker the bad news; Pharaoh was going to take his life. Joseph's predictions came to pass. Unfortunately, the chief butler forgot all about Joseph until two years later, when Pharaoh of Egypt had two troubling dreams and inquired of all his wise men and magicians to interpret them.

Pharaoh's dreams were so puzzling that he stayed awake after the second recurring dream and demanded answers—immediately! No one in Pharaoh's court could help him, and he was highly upset and even considered putting them all to death. Then the chief butler told Pharaoh how he was wrong in forgetting to tell him about the gifted Joseph, who had accurately interpreted his and the former chief baker's dreams.

- Pharaoh summoned Joseph, and they quickly cleaned and shaved him and made him presentable to stand before Pharaoh.
- Pharaoh repeated his two dreams to Joseph, who humbly stated, "I cannot do it." Joseph replied to Pharaoh, "But God will give Pharaoh the answer he desires" (Gen. 41:16 NIV).
- Pharaoh shared his first dream (Gen. 41:17–21). He saw seven well-fed cows coming out of the river and grazing in the meadows. But then seven ill cows came after them and ate the seven fatted cows. After eating the well-favored cows, the ill cows still looked as sickly as they appeared at the beginning.
- Pharaoh then shared his second dream (Gen. 41:22–24). He saw seven healthy ears of corn come from one stalk, and then seven deprived, drought-thin ears of corn came and ate the seven healthy ears of corn. A major key to both of these dreams is that the ill-fated remained the same after devouring the healthy ones.

Joseph stated that God gave him the ability to interpret dreams, and he shared with Pharaoh what was about to happen in the near future. Joseph not only accurately interpreted the dreams but also shared that Pharaoh's rapidly recurring dreams represented something that would happen very soon.

Joseph said the dreams were just alike. The seven favored cows and the seven healthy stalks of corn represented the same factors, while the seven sickly cows were also matched with the seven drought-like thin stalks of corn. The groups of seven represented seven years. The healthy seven represented seven years of favorable conditions that would prosper the land and its ability to produce. The seven unhealthy groups represented seven years of famine-like conditions that would wipe away the previous seven years of abundance. This famine would destroy both produce and livestock.

Joseph was given immediate wisdom from the Lord on what Pharaoh needed to do to overcome the years of unbearable bad conditions. He shared how the pharaoh needed to appoint a man of great discernment and business savvy over this massive project of labor and rescue. Joseph elaborated on how each prosperous year had to be well managed by taking 20 percent (one-fifth) of the bumper crops and storing them in and around the cities.

Pharaoh was greatly impressed with Joseph. "So Pharaoh asked his officials, 'Can we find anyone else like this man so obviously filled with the spirit of God?' Then Pharaoh said to Joseph, 'Since God has revealed the meaning of the dreams to you, clearly no one else is as intelligent or wise as you are'" (Gen. 41:38–39 NLT).

Pharaoh then appointed Joseph to take the charge of the land. This was Joseph's third promotion in Egypt, where he began as a slave! Joseph was not only given the authority of being second-in-command of Egypt, but he was also appointed to be in charge of all Pharaoh's personal goods. Along with his new appointment as land supervisor and Pharaoh's personal steward/vizier, it was commanded, "Not one hand could move in Egypt without Joseph's approval" (Gen. 41:44 NLT). This meant that *everything* under Pharaoh's governmental control had to be approved by Joseph: the priesthood, the military, the courts, everything. Pharaoh felt so relieved and fulfilled that he even took the ring from his hand and placed it on Joseph's—a sign of equality, respect, and authority throughout all the land. After giving him the best garments made of the finest linens, he also put a gold chain like no other around Joseph's neck. But Pharaoh was not finished.

As mentioned, Joseph was promoted three times, but the fourth promotion is often overlooked when discussing his life. The pharaoh arranged for Joseph, who was now thirty years old, to be married to Asenath, the Egyptian daughter of the priest of On. *This fourth and final exaltation is so over-the-top!* Please take a moment to absorb this kind of turnaround in Joseph's life, as well as understand that he suddenly surpassed every personal and cultural bias all in one day.

After all the years of suffering, betrayal by his brothers, who he naively thought honestly loved him; enslavement with shackles around his ankles at age seventeen; traveling about 350 miles away from home across a ferocious desert to a foreign land; being torn from his beloved father and youngest brother of his biological mother; and despite performing well in the households of his masters, Joseph still was nothing more than a slave. If this story had ended right there, it would simply be an astonishing story of redemptive love and mercy shown to one who had been rejected, lied about, and overlooked.

We don't have to look too far into today's society to find a prospective of this redemptive love and mercy. A recent, modern day historical exaltation occurred in the life of South African President Nelson Mandela. The story of this profound civil rights leader, who was imprisoned for twenty-seven years in the racist society of apartheid in South Africa, only to eventually become the president of the nation, is simply mind-blowing. His story showed the richness of humility and the providential works of the spirit world and its Creator—not seen but manifested. It should also be noted that Joseph had a twenty-seven-year stint, as well, from the time he was sold, until the time the famine ended.

Like Mandela, Joseph was a prisoner without voice or due process. Let's be reminded that he was a Hebrew slave in hostile territory. Hebrews or Jews were not looked upon as favored people during that time. They were considered nomads, who were shepherds. The Scriptures clearly state how the Egyptian society looked down on herdsmen (Gen. 43:31–33, 46:34 AMP). For Joseph to rise to such stature and be exalted as one of the most powerful men in the world (next to the leader of the most powerful nation on the Earth at the time, Pharaoh himself) is absolutely breathtaking exaltation!

The story does not end there. Out of his fourth promotion, Joseph's wife bore him two sons, Manasseh and Ephraim. They were so named because they brought pure joy to Joseph. Things were bountiful and finally looking up for Joseph like never before!

CHAPTER 3

A FAMILY RESTORED

Those seven years were blissful for Joseph, as we have seen. But Joseph was unable to rest on his esteemed laurels, as Pharaoh's second critical apportionment was yet to come to pass. As Joseph predicted, seven years of famine followed those prosperous years of plenty. Fortunately, Joseph's dream interpretation allowed for proper planning for the famine.

After the first year of famine, Joseph's family back home began to suffer. His father, Jacob, heard there was plenty of food in Egypt, so he ordered his sons to caravan there with money to buy food. When the sons arrived, they had to report to Joseph. He was unrecognizable to his brothers, as we can imagine, decked out in Egyptian official-type clothing, a custom hairdo, possibly wearing accessories, including makeup, and now speaking in the Egyptian language. Plus, he was now twenty-two years older. His voice had matured, his physique was enlarged, and his educational background and experience had him behaving at a totally different level than his prior nomadic behavior and customs.

In an effort to better observe his brothers, Joseph spoke through an interpreter, acting as though he did not understand their language. Joseph's brothers engaged him, awestruck by his regal presence. Joseph accused his brothers of coming into the land as spies. He used this tactic to find out more about his family, which he had not seen in decades. Joseph spoke with a tough demeanor as he probed his brothers for information about their family background. They told him that their father, Jacob, was old but still holding on and that they had a younger brother named Benjamin, who was dear to their father.

After the interrogation was over, Joseph agreed to allow his brothers to purchase food, and he even fed them. But to make sure they were telling the truth about his father and youngest brother, Joseph demanded that one of the brothers, Simeon, stay in Egypt while the others returned home and then brought back Benjamin. Joseph told them this would prove they were telling the truth.

But in fact, Joseph just longed to see Benjamin, his full-blooded youngest brother of his biological parents, Jacob and Rachel. On the way back home, the brothers discovered that inside their sacks of food was all the money they had paid to purchase the food. The sons of Jacob were smote in their hearts, as they dared to consider what would now happen to Simeon, who, by the way, was imprisoned in the same prison where Joseph was once held. This was Joseph's plan, however. He secretly had all the money returned to them.

Jacob regretted the moment he granted his sons permission to leave again on yet another expedition to Egypt. The famine was just too severe, and both human and animal livelihood was at stake. This time the brothers were carrying double the money than on their previous trip, to honor the apparent mistake that was made wherein the money for the first food purchase was found in their sacks.

More precious than the money, Jacob was sending Benjamin, his last memorial trophy of Rachel and a grievous memory of Joseph. Jacob had no other choice; he had to submit to his son Judah's plea. Judah promised Jacob he would watch over Benjamin and keep him safe.

When they arrived in Egypt the second time, the brothers quickly made it known to the government official, Joseph, that they had returned with their brother, Benjamin. They also explained that the money from the previous purchase had never been removed from their sacks.

Joseph greeted his brothers with a special dinner prepared just for them. Simeon was released from prison, and a happy reunion occurred. To the brothers' amazement, Joseph sat with them at the table and had everyone seated in their exact birth order!

Joseph's longing for Benjamin bled through when he gave each brother a healthy meal but gave Benjamin five times as much food—a feast fit for a king. Wisely, the older brothers said nothing about the perceived favoritism.

Joseph continued his payback for his years of mistreatment, however. He commanded the steward of his house to place his silver cup in Benjamin's sack before his brothers headed back home, feeling hopeful and fulfilled. After journeying several uneventful miles toward their home in Canaan, suddenly Pharaoh's chariots came roaring down the road, headed directly toward Jacob's sons.

The head soldier commanded the brothers to stop. He ordered a search of the sacks of grain because the master's silver cup was missing. The brothers chorused that this must be a mistake, relating that they had even returned the money that was mistakenly left in their sacks the last time.

Joseph's silver cup was found in Benjamin's sack. The brothers were astonished and horrified. They ripped their clothes in dejection and traveled back into Egypt, under arrest by the pharaoh's cavalry.

Joseph hovered over his brothers, and they believed their lives were now in danger because they were considered criminals. They stretched out before him to beg for mercy, as Judah spoke on behalf of himself and his brothers.

Judah shared that he knew the almighty God had judged them for their wickedness, and he declared that they were all now Pharaoh's servants. Joseph stated that only the guilty person, Benjamin, in whose sack the silver chalice was found, would be forever required to be his servant. Joseph gave the other brothers permission to leave.

Judah pleaded and begged for the return of Benjamin, sharing how their father's life was wrapped up in this boy and that Jacob would surely die if anything was to happen to Benjamin or if he couldn't see him again. Judah explained how his father did not even want them to travel with Benjamin because the young man was Jacob's token memory of his late wife Rachel and his long-gone son, Joseph. Judah even pleaded to be allowed to change places with his younger brother.

Joseph refused the request. If the brothers were to do any more business with him, he must keep Benjamin as his servant.

Judah began to wail. How could he ever face his father and tell him that Benjamin had been imprisoned forever, never to be seen again? Judah told Joseph that the brothers would lose their father, as Jacob would surely go to the grave quickly, as his heart would be ripped beyond repair (Gen. 44).

Hard-nosed Joseph could take it no more. He was overcome with remorse and longing for his father, Jacob. Tears streamed down Joseph's face, and he commanded his guards to leave the room immediately. He wept loud and ferociously, and all the house of Pharaoh heard him.

Joseph composed himself enough to reveal himself to his brothers, and they were so shocked they could hardly move. Joseph begged them to come near, as they were frightened after what they'd done to him. He was powerful now, and they had once sold him into slavery!

Amazingly, Joseph's heart was full of forgiveness. He shared with his brothers how, after they sold him into slavery, God preserved him for their deliverance, along with the deliverance of the rest of mankind. He explained the terrible plague on the land would last five more years and that he wanted them to go and get Jacob and all their households and return to Egypt to live with him.

Joseph sent wagons, Egyptian manpower, and supplies with the message, "Tell my father about all the honor accorded me in Egypt and about everything you have seen. And bring my father down here quickly" (Gen. 45:13 NIV). Joseph fell on Benjamin's neck, crying tears of joy and relief. Their reunion was no longer a dream; it actually happened! Joseph then hugged and kissed all his brothers from his treacherous past.

News spread throughout the land, and Pharaoh was pleased when he heard of this glorious reunion. Then Pharaoh insisted that Joseph's family move to Egypt, stating that he would provide them with everything necessary for the journey and safe return (Gen. 45). Pharaoh gave the brothers everything they could possibly need for the journey, including changes of garments. He gave Benjamin three hundred silver coins and five changes of clothing.

Joseph knew it was not just about their safe journey but also about a happy survival, so he sent ten male donkeys burdened down with the finer things of Egypt and ten female donkeys loaded down with grain, bread, and meat, just for Jacob.

Joseph concludes on a firm note of instruction for his brothers, telling them not to go back fighting and blaming each other for separating him from family and causing their father so much pain (Gen. 45:24).

When they finally arrived back home, there was music and celebration throughout the area. The brothers told Jacob that Joseph was not only still alive but was governor over all the land of Egypt. Please understand that Egypt was the mightiest nation on the earth at that time and had been for over a thousand years.

Jacob nearly fainted. He could hardly believe what his sons had told him until he saw the wagons and supplies they'd brought from Egypt. The moment was so surreal that Jacob hastily said, "I will go and see him before I die" (Gen. 45:28 NKJV).

Jacob, his children, and their families and households headed to Egypt. They brought back all their goods and animals, and their wives journeyed along with them in chariots. Altogether, Jacob had sixty-six in his household, not including Joseph, his sons, or himself. Jacob stopped along the way in Beersheba to worship with animal sacrifices.

The Almighty visited him in "visions of the night" (Gen. 46:1–2 NLT). God informed Jacob that He was behind this, so he should rest in peace. He said, "I will make you into a great nation. I will bring you back surely again." (Gen. 46:3–4 NLT).

With blessed assurance, a total of seventy Hebrews had now arrived safely in Egypt. Joseph went out to Goshen in his glorious chariot to meet his father. With tears of joy, he embraced his father and wept on his shoulders. The long-awaited separation was over. Jacob reiterated how he could now die in peace as he beheld the face of his dear son, Joseph. Joseph then briefed his father on how to greet and address the pharaoh of Egypt. Then he took five of his brothers and Jacob to meet Pharaoh.

As was customary, Pharaoh asked the brothers some questions first. "What is your occupation?" (Gen. 47:3). As Joseph had instructed them, they told Pharaoh that they were shepherds who raised and traded in domesticated animals. Pharaoh then told them he wanted them to dwell on the best land and raise their cattle and flocks along with his. Joseph then brought in his father, Jacob, who blessed Pharaoh, according to his custom.

Pharaoh asked him, "How old are you?" (Gen. 47:8–9). Jacob informed him that he was 130 years old but was not many years compared to the days of his forefathers. Jacob then blessed Pharaoh again, upon leaving his courts, and Joseph ushered his brothers to the best grazing land in all of Egypt.

The famine continued and the storyline deepened, but the nation survived certain destruction, under the leadership of Joseph's wisdom.

CHAPTER 4

DIGGING FOR PROOF

Considering the richness of Joseph's suffering and exaltation, it is no wonder his life story is beloved unto this day. Even in the midst of all the differences between the beliefs of Islam, Judaism, and Christianity, this story is highly valued as true and serves as a peaceful reminder of what can happen if the true and living God is with you. No matter what has happened, a silver lining of hope can still be discovered.

Some may ask, "Is the Bible even true?" You may wonder if it is just my belief as a religious clergyman or if perhaps actual proof of its validity exists. The story sounds good, but can it hold up as more than simply a fictional story of inspiration?

Legitimately, the Bible has never been found to be wrong in its own right in the capable hands of proper representation of knowledgeable scholars. The authentic findings and studies of the Dead Sea Scrolls, discovered in 1947 by a Bedouin shepherd boy, underscores how textual reliability was strictly adhered to for over two thousand years. Science affirms the Scriptures when proper scholarship and open-mindedness are applied.

This one law remains constant in understanding the Scriptures: you must believe in an almighty God who can perform miracles and do the impossible. Without this insight, no matter how plain and clearly anyone spells it out for you, you will stumble and miss the keys of truth necessary to prepare you for an eventual relationship with Him.

I *did not* write this book for only religious people. I wrote it for whoever wants to read it and consider its validity. If inspiration is the best thing you can find in this text, so be it. Because of all the extensive work of archaeologists and studies in Egyptology, things have surfaced to shed a brighter light on the reality of the ancient phenomenon named *Joseph.*

Did the children of Israel (Jacob) ever have a place of prominence or dwelling in the land of Egypt? Is the story of Moses and the Jewish Passover true? Without Joseph, there is no Jewish settlement with an initial peaceful coexistence in the land of Egypt. Joseph was the man who made all of this possible.

Here are just a few of the many discoveries that provide further legitimacy of the 3,800 year-old story regarding Joseph of Egypt.

The Discovery of a Tomb of a Wealthy Yemenite

Text written on the stone tablet reveals that this woman was a person of wealth in that she had plenty of substance and a steward to serve her household. The inscription describes a famine-like condition and an appeal to a man called Joseph during this apparent time of desperation.

The story from Genesis we discussed in chapter 3 reveals that the famine was widespread, and people traveled from all over Africa and the Mediterranean to purchase food for their homelands.

> In the name O God, the God of Hamyar, I Tajah, the daughter of Dzu Shefar, sent my steward to Joseph, And he delaying to return to me, I sent my hand maid With a measure of silver, to bring me back a measure of flour: And not being able to procure it, I sent her with a measure of gold: And not being able to procure it, I sent her with a measure of pearls: And not being able to procure it, I

commanded them to be ground: And finding no profit in them, I am shut up here. Whosoever may hear of it, let him commiserate me; And should any woman adorn herself with an ornament from my ornaments, may she die with no other than my death.[20]

The inscription tells that story of a suffering, yet wealthy, Arab woman. It is no coincidence that Joseph's waterway, used to prevent the drying of Lake Quaran, exists under that name and that the famine predicted by him did indeed take place. It is significant that the Yemenite Arab woman addressed her complaint to Joseph, showing that he held the high position the Bible tells us about.

The Nineteenth-Century Discovery of a Marble Tablet Found Ancient Southern Saudi Arabia (Current-Day Yemen)

We dwelt at ease in this castle a long tract of time; nor had we a desire but for the region-lord of the vineyard. Hundreds of camels returned to us each day at evening, their eye pleasant to behold in their resting-places. And twice the number of our camels were our sheep, in comeliness like white does, and also the slow moving kine. We dwelt in this castle seven years of good life— how difficult for memory its description! Then came years barren and burnt up: when one evil year had passed away, Then came another to succeed it. And we became as though we had never seen a glimpse of good. They died and neither foot nor hoof remained. Thus fares it with him who renders not thanks to God: His footsteps fail not to be blotted out from his dwelling.[21]

---

[20]   Grant, 1991.
[21]   Grant, 1999.

The Discovery of a Special Palace and Garden/ Tomb in the Ancient Land of Goshen

> So Joseph died, being one hundred and ten years old; and they embalmed him, and he was put in a coffin in Egypt. (Gen. 50:26 NKJV).

David Rohl, the famed biblical archaeologist, and his team discovered what was believed to be a large palace structure in the area of Goshen, where the story from Genesis shares that Joseph's family was given permission to live by Pharaoh.

About three hundred years prior, in the area of P-Ramses (the ancient area of Goshen), there was a civilization called Avaris, where there is much proof that the people had Semitic (of ancient Hebrew origins) tools, relics, and burial rituals, mixed with Egyptian culture tools. There was discovered a palace structure that was not for an Egyptian pharaoh, though it had twelve colonnades, which could have been significant to symbolize Joseph and his brothers. The palace was befitting of a dignified official. What was also striking was that the palace had two enlarged living spaces, like apartments, in the front, which also fits the story of Joseph, who raised his two sons, Manasseh and Ephraim, and their separate households.

There was a tomb topped with a pyramid in the back of the palace-like structure, where there apparently was a garden with a broken tomb entrance. A statue was also in the area, and the statue was smashed in the area of the head, yet color remained on the statue, depicting a type of robe of a Semitic style. The hair on the statue had a reddish tone as well, and the style appears to be of the Semitic ancient culture. In one hand, an Egyptian rod of authority could be detected. This gave tremendous proof that the person was of significant status as an Egyptian official during his tenure. David Rohl's belief is that this was the tomb of Joseph and the tomb was carefully broken into to remove the body or bones of Joseph at the time of Moses and the

This reconstruction of Joseph serves as a composite from the remains of the statue that was found at the archeological site, found near Avaris in northeast Egypt. The statue was outside of a garden tomb, and on the property of a large palace like structure. Along with Hebrew artifacts and the colored robe, signs seem to point towards the Biblical character of Joseph, after his days of being the right hand man of Pharaoh. These findings were first identified by Manfred Beitak and further excavated by David Rohl and his exploration team. Photo accredited to David Rohl.

exodus.[22] Yet Rohl commented that those hating Joseph and his people could have ruined the statue once they left the land of Egypt some three hundred years later.[23]

---

[22] *Https://www.youtube.com/watch?v=lm9ATLhkujY&list=TLdw_ YGuRWXwVjMbjbuoLFnZFdT_i6wnCQ.* Booth, J. [producer]. N.d. BBC/ Discovery Channel. Web.

[23] Ibid.

The findings of Rohl and his research team were not original, as this excavation research was previously confirmed by Manfred Beitak of the Austrian Archaelogical Institute of Cairo, Egypt, from the 1960s.[24] He believes the Hyskos were rulers of the twelfth dynasty and that Joseph possibly served three pharoahs: Senuret II, Senuret III, and Amenemhat III.[25] He shares the same views of the tomb and statue findings as David Rohl.[26]

The Current Dispute of the Tomb of Joseph, One of Israel's Most Holy Sites

For decades now, in the midst of the struggle between the Israelis and the Palestinians, the tomb of Joseph has been in the forefront of physical confrontations. Though debated, it is highly favorable that the tomb is the actual memorial site of the bones of Joseph, where they were actually buried and have been memorialized over the centuries. The modern name of the town is Nablus, but the ancient name for the area is Shechem. The tomb is only 325 yards northwest of the ancient historical site of Jacob's Well. This area is in the West Bank, which serves as a dividing line between the ancient territories of the tribes Ephraim and Manassas, divided under the leadership of Joshua. Manassas and Ephraim were sons of equal inheritance, along with the other sons of Jacob.

John Elder recorded the following in his book, *Prophets, Idols, and Diggers*:

> In the last verses of Genesis it is told how Joseph adjured
> his relatives to take his bones back to Canaan whenever

---

[24] Beitak, Manfred. "Comments on the Exodus." Egypt, Israel, Sinai: Archaeological and Historical Relationships in the Biblical Period." Diss. Tel Aviv University, 1987. Web.

[25] Ibid.

[26] Rohl, 1997.

God should restore them to their original home, and in Joshua 24:32 it is told how his body was indeed brought to Palestine and buried in Shechem. For centuries there was a tomb at Shechem reverenced as the Tomb of Joseph. A few years ago the tomb was opened. It was found to contain a body mummified according to the Egyptian custom, and in the tomb, among other things, was a sword of the kind worn by Egyptian officials.[27]

A Man-Made Lake/Canal that Preserves Joseph's Legacy Today

This is one of my favorite pieces of evidence. Studies of Tanzania and Mount Kilimanjaro's ice cores, which feed the Nile River with water, have revealed that a terrible drought occurred in the region about 3,600 years ago or approximately in the twelfth dynasty of the pharaohs. This proximity aligns with the time of Joseph's reign and service with the pharaoh.

One of the most fertile areas was land around Lake Quarun or Moeris. This lake feeds off the Nile, and during times of drought, the area suffered as a tributary. But between 1850 BC and 1650 BC, a canal was built to prevent drought conditions, allowing the land to be constantly nurtured all year long. This canal was built with such perfection and engineering that it still functions today in the original fashion.

There is no official record to determine who built the canal, but for thousands of years now, it has been called *Bahr Yussef.* The name is an Arabic transliteration, but the English transliteration means, *the waterway of Joseph!* The root name of Joseph (*Yosef*) is Hebraic. So, in the northern part of Africa, where the Egyptians were the dominant rulers of the Mediterranean and the known world during this period,

---

[27] Elder, 1960

you have a memorialized Hebraic name of a disrespected, lower-class people. This can only be true if the person named *Yussef* was well respected, far beyond the norm.

> "And they set on for him by himself, and for them by themselves, and for the Egyptians, which did eat with him, by themselves: because the Egyptians might not eat bread with the Hebrews; for that is an abomination unto the Egyptians. (Gen. 43:32 KJV)

I soberly share with you that this *Yussef* is none other than Joseph of Egypt, Jacob's son, a man still revered by the major three religions of our day: Judaism, Christianity, and Islam. Even the engineering ability of the waterway speaks of futuristic insight that protects a land ahead of a preemptive crisis. The story speaks of Joseph being given full reign to oversee his perceptions in interpreting the pharaoh's dreams. He had seven years to prepare and take on this massive construction project.

But that's not all that points to this phenomenal leader. In further archeological findings, the foundational ruins of what appears to be an extensive, elaborate labyrinth is found in this same area. Excavations revealed that this labyrinth was so immense in capacity of storage and acreage that it would have served well as a headquarters for Pharaoh and his government.

Herodotus's Egyptian Labyrinth

Herodotus was an infamous historian of ancient Greece. He lived around 450 BC, and his statue is found in many places. His records, though thought to be embellished and even fictitious in places, overall provide a working knowledge and foundation of the times in which he lived. In a description, he records what he thought was a labyrinth, a mazelike structure, so huge it was like one of the seven wonders of the world.[28] Located in Egypt near the waterway of Joseph lies the ruins of what Herodotus thought surpassed the engineering beauty of pyramids that he describes as such:

> "It has twelve covered courts—six in a row facing north, six south—the gates of the one range exactly fronting the gates of the other. Inside, the building is of two stories and contains three thousand rooms, of which half are underground, and the other half directly above them. I was taken through the rooms in the upper storey, so what I shall say of them is from my own observation, but the underground ones I can speak of only from report, because the Egyptians in charge refused to let me see them, as they contain the tombs of the kings who built the labyrinth, and also the tombs of the sacred crocodiles. The upper rooms, on the contrary, I did actually see, and it is hard to believe that they are the work of men; the baffling and intricate passages from room to room and from court to court were an endless wonder to me, as we passed from a courtyard into rooms, from rooms into galleries, from galleries into more rooms and thence into yet more courtyards. The roof of every chamber, courtyard, and gallery is, like the walls of stone. The walls are covered with carved figures, and each court is exquisitely built of white marble and surrounded by a colonnade.[29]

Known as the father of history, Herodotus claimed that he saw the layout of this building and felt that if you had put together all of the great buildings of ancient Greece, it still would have

---

[28] Herodotus. *The History of Herodotus.* #2707 ed. Vol. 1. N.p.: Gutenburg Files-Updated, 1/25/2013. Histories II. ISO-8859-1.

[29] Michalowski, 1968.

been inferior to what he personally observed.[30] He acknowledged that, according to the stories of the native people, the lake was man-made, and the labyrinth seemed to be situated in the very location that was still providing a favorable ecological balance to the area.[31]

Even though it is believed that the labyrinth was added onto over the years by the various pharaohs of the ancient dynasties, the oldest inscription on behalf of the pharaohs is that of Amenemhat III. David Rohl, in his explorations recorded in his book *Pharaohs and Kings: A Biblical Conquest*, had serious reconsiderations of the timeline of the pharaohs, while providing proof of why he thought Joseph possibly served as Pharaoh's vizier, under his rule.[32]

With the evidence of the historical and physical reality of the man-made lake Bahr Yussef, the huge labyrinth with more rooms and storage space than imaginable, the oldest name of the pharaohs being that of Amenemhat III, and the approximate time of drought conditions attested by archaeologists by the Nile flooding for a seven-year period, seems to fit the biblical address of wisdom and vision provided by Joseph. Joseph stated right after he interpreted the dreams of Pharaoh that he needed to appoint someone to oversee the seven years of prosperity, while saving 20 percent of the produce and harvest of the land (Gen. 41:34).

The labyrinth would have served well for the needed national storage center, where the likes of the nation of Egypt and other foreigners came to do business during the crisis years of severe famine and drought.

So much more proof of the Israelite occupation in key areas of Egypt—such as tombs, recorded stories, inscriptions on ancient tablets of recorded history, and more—could be included here. I only want to provide enough documentation for readers to

---

[30] Herodotus. *The History of Herodotus*. #2707 ed. Vol. 1. N.p.: Gutenburg Files-Updated, 1/25/2013. Histories II. ISO-8859-1.
[31] Ibid.
[32] Rohl, 1997.

understand and to allow for their own research of sources. The biblical account holds its own in the midst of differing opinions. I would not be surprised if additional affirming discoveries of this tremendous hero surface in the next couple of years. Enough evidence is presented here to affirm that the biblical account has merit and can be trusted.

CHAPTER 5

DREAMS BEYOND THIS WORLD

Even with all the archaeological proof that surrounds the reality of Joseph's life, it still requires faith to simply *believe*. Because God is invisible to the naked eye, we have to believe in our hearts that He exists and is able to perform as the Creator with all power, knowledge, and experience. This simple backdrop of faith brings Joseph and other biblical heroes into our world. In the story, it was not just Joseph who had faith. Others, including the pharaoh himself, had to exercise faith. The evidence of this was when the pharaoh said, "Can we find such a man as this, in whom is the Spirit of God?" (Genesis 41:38 RSV).

It is in this spirit of thought that we can move forward. We must understand that the troubling dreams were given to Pharaoh by God, and they spoke of urgency—something that was going to happen in the near future. According to the Scriptures, when governmental leaders and heads of nations were given dreams and their wise men, religious priests, or counselors could not interpret them, they would call on a religiously endowed person who was known to have a relationship with the true and living God. Although many national leaders worshipped idols and gods of mythology, when an urgent answer was needed, they didn't care whether the interpreter of the dream worshipped a different deity. Pharaoh also did not care about Joseph's status as a slave. His only concern was receiving answers about his mind-boggling dreams.

If God is the Creator of all things, then He also possesses all knowledge concerning that which He made. Joseph was the gifted one, but the giver of the gift was God, who gave him the knowledge to do what he could do. The wisdom God gave him was not just the knowledge of facts but also precise, arranged knowledge. The gift of wisdom is knowing how to put things in order and arranging it to make it work at a premium.

This gift, however, did not originate with Joseph. His great-grandfather Abraham had the same endowment, although Joseph had that extra *something*. God was prophesying—speaking of the future—when He gave Joseph the dream about the sheaves. That is why Joseph, in his immaturity, was so upbeat when telling others about his dreams.

Let's reiterate Joseph's first dream. The first dream showed his sheaves standing up while the other eleven sheaves bowed down to his. Joseph and his brothers understood it as Joseph ruling over them, and they showed their disapproval of his perceived arrogance. The second dream portrayed Joseph as a star, and the eleven stars (his brothers) along with the sun and moon gave obeisance to him. Jacob honestly thought the sun represented him and the moon represented his wife, Leah. I beg to differ. No disrespect meant toward Jacob, but he was a man who had flaws, like all humanity has flaws. He was God's man and chosen vessel, but the biblical record indicates that he did not always interpret things accurately. For instance, not only was he fooled by the Joseph's coat which was stained with animal blood, but even when he was reunited with Joseph, he felt death was near, though he lived another seventeen years!

Let's consider how the children were birthed by four different women; two (Bilhah and Zilpah) were surrogate mothers who were considered cultural property. These two served under Rachel and Leah. Rachel was the birth mother of Joseph, but she passed away during his baby brother Benjamin's birth. In the biblical record, and even in the evolutionary theory of planetary development, the sun and moon do not give birth to the stars. Thus, I believe the second dream was deeper and more complex.

Scientifically, the sun and the moon are greater than the stars in our galaxy because they direct the movement and rotations of the earth while the other planets compliment the earth. The sun and moon direct time and seasons while the other stars decorate the backdrop of the earth's habitation. The sun and moon bowing down to Joseph indicated time and seasons and that the Creator was going to use this process to bring about this projected authority that Joseph would have over his family. By text, Jacob never bowed down to Joseph, but in fact, at Jacob's blessing of Joseph's sons, and at his death, Joseph bowed in subjection to his father.

The sun and the moon *are not* parents or originators of the other planets. I know some people might disagree, according to the evolutionary big bang theory relative to the origination of the earth. But even if the earth came out of the sun, it does not fit the considered interpretation that the sun and moon also bowed down to Joseph's star. In short, the interpretation is more long-term and broad in scope than what Jacob first perceived in his heart and mind. The Scripture states that Jacob considered what the last dream actually meant and was pondering it, because he knew Joseph had this unique gift of knowing what would happen before things took place (Gen. 37:11).

If we want to consider what was actually being communicated from the heavens to Joseph about himself and the destiny of his family, we need to go back to the creation story and recollect what it states about the "sun and the moon." We find this written in the book of Genesis:

> Then God said, "Let there be lights in the firmament of the heavens to divide the day from the night; and let them be for signs and seasons, and for days and years; and let them be for lights in the firmament of the heavens to give light

on the Earth"; and it was so. Then God made two great lights: the greater light to rule the day, and the lesser light to rule the night. *He made* the stars also. God set them in the firmament of the heavens to give light on the Earth, and to rule over the day and over the night, and to divide the light from the darkness. And God saw that *it was* good. So the evening and the morning were the fourth day. (Gen. 1:14–19 NKJV)

Several points need to be mentioned here. The Scriptures designate the sun and moon as two great lights; one greater and one lesser, respectively. On the fourth day of Creation, we can see four purposes for the lights and stars:

1. **Signs**
2. **Seasons**
3. **Days**
4. **Years**

The sun, moon, and stars were made for signs—marks of distinction to be remembered as a special moment in time. These signs were to embrace the miraculous as well as the natural order of things and to serve as omens and/or warnings to mankind and his elect.

The planetary system also serves as seasons, referred to in Hebrew as *mow' ed*, which is defined as a special time or place designated for meeting or a coming together of the people for appointed times.[33] We recognize the four seasons as spring, summer, fall, and winter. Today we rely on written and established calendars for times and dates, such as holidays. But in ancient times, they relied on the stars and their locales for acknowledgments and sacred considerations. The moon in its orbit plays a key role today in determining a full monthly cycle. The moon has four main phases: full moon, half moon, and

---

[33] http://lexiconcordance.com/hebrew/4150.html.

two quarters toward the east or west side. This rotation of precise movement takes twenty nine and a half days.[34]

We see on the fourth day of creation the four purposes of the sun, moon, and stars, plus the placement of seasons, of which there are also four. Depending upon your location, whether you are close to the equator or at the distant poles, there are distinguishing points of reference that establish the time and season that is about to come.

Considering the *Law of First Mention*,[35] Genesis is the first place in the Scriptures where the number *four* is mentioned. What we see and believe by faith is that God's creation dictates the type of Creator He is. This is not just westernized Christianity; the eastern religions and the Native Americans (the first nation tribes) recognize that nature speaks of and is connected to our Designer-Creator. In the same way we evaluate an artist or professional designer, the object made has the imprint of its designer. Recognized painters and artists have their mindset immersed in their works. That's what sets them apart. We can say that about leaders, speakers, and authors of any kind. See, the truth remains; we were made in the image and likeness of our Creator (Gen. 1:26–27).

Let's revisit this as we consider sequence and pattern. On the fourth day, we see four distinct purposes for the sun, moon, and stars. This is not by accident. We are called to believe, by faith, that there is a purpose for everything; however, many times we are limited in our thinking concerning what we perceive as the purpose for a thing (Eccl. 3:1).

The fourth day is a double 4, in that it is the fourth day with four distinct purposes. Like the dreams Joseph had prior to meeting the pharaoh, which consequently prepared him for his primary purpose, so it is with this law of first mention concerning the number 4. Joseph had two dreams back to back, and it was not long after that his life changed forever; his brothers betrayed him. Joseph interpreted the

---

[34] http://www.stargazing.net/david/moon/index29days.html.
[35] http://www.biblicalresearch.info/page48.html.

two dreams of the butler and the baker, and in three days, their fate was determined. When the pharaoh had two dreams back to back, Joseph became aware of the urgency of what was about to take place. Joseph was now not just a gifted man—he could detect the urgency of situations.

Joseph was born a double 4. The sun and moon also have a double 4 relationship regarding their purpose with the earth. Joseph and his brothers are the fourth generation of Abraham. One of the Ten Commandments states:

> You shall not bow down to them or worship them; for I, the LORD your God, am a jealous God, punishing the children for the sin of the parents to the third and fourth generation of those who hate me, but showing love to a thousand generations of those who love me and keep my commandments. (Ex. 20:5–6 NIV)

There are several points to be made here. I am referencing the spirit of the text, not the whole meaning of the text, which is so exceedingly important. I want you to see the depth and importance of how God sees the third, even the fourth, dimension of something. There is the blessing of obedience and the curse of disobedience. Joseph chose the blessing of obedience, and we can see where it took him. Even a number to its third or fourth power versus the singular number represents a profound difference. The number 3 by itself remains at that value, but 3 to the fourth power (3^4) becomes 81 (3 x 3 x 3 x 3 = 81)!

God is not jealous, as in envious, like the immature thinking of the world. The word *jealous* is connected to His immeasurable love for us, not the things we possess, which, by the way, He also provides.

Joseph was not only the by-product of Abraham's lineage; he was also born of his father's first love choice—Rachel! Jacob fell in love and wanted to marry only Rachel, but she ended up as the fourth of four women to have a child with Jacob. Unfortunately,

Rachel eventually lost her life giving birth to their second child, Benjamin. This unexpected, seemingly backward birth circumstance caused Joseph to be a *double 4*. Joseph was a double 4 from his father Abraham, to his mother Rachel.

Is this starting to add up for you? Hopefully so, because Joseph's name actually means "to add up or add upon."[36] This is so much more than mere coincidence; this is destiny. Joseph was highly endowed to make a difference in the most excellent way. Everything he touched increased in one way or another. The first dream about him and his brothers was connected to harvesting—bundles of sheaves of a perceived wheat or barley harvest. That's right! He had the Midas touch, in that everything he touched turned to gold.

So what are we seeing? Joseph, who is a mystical double 4, has a second dream about the two mainstays, the sun and the moon, which were made or formed and completed on the fourth day of our present creative order. I have been shown that this is much bigger than previously considered. The number 4 denotes universal effects, creative works, and material completion. The second dream Joseph had about the sun and moon giving in or submitting to him was about how these two mighty timekeepers would serve the purpose of why Joseph was even born.

The Creator—the God of Abraham, Isaac, and Jacob—revealed this dream to Joseph: the sun and the moon have a 400-degree relationship, a strange but beautiful alliance that was not known among men. This 400-degree relationship is solidified when a total eclipse is encountered. In a total eclipse, the moon fits directly into the sun's circular disc and causes almost a complete block out of the sun's light for a minute or so. This angled phenomenon is made possible by the fact that the sun is approximately 400 times larger than the moon, yet it is also four hundred times farther away. From earth's view, it is like a large beach ball fitting perfectly into the

---

[36] http://www.biblecharts.org/oldtestament/interestingfactsaboutjoseph.pdf.

outside perimeter of an American penny, only because of the exact distance between them.[37]

I first heard this ironic analogy from Dr. Guillermo Gonzalez's DVD presentation, *The Privileged Planet*, and from his same-titled book. He elaborates, saying:

> There's a striking convergence of rare properties that allow people on Earth to witness perfect solar eclipses … total eclipses are possible because the sun is four hundred times larger than the moon, but it's also four hundred times farther away. It's that incredible coincidence that creates a perfect match.[38]

I believe this signifies a designed relationship, as the sun, moon, and stars were coordinated for the earth's habitable conditions. Some may say, according to evolution, the earth has been habitable for millions of years, but I am directly referring to the renewed habitation the Scriptures indicate; the fact that the sun and moon were shaped into a correlating, ongoing cycle that determined life existed eternally on earth. This 400/400 relationship between the sun and the moon is based upon the axis degree angles in conjunction with the earth. According to the Hebrew mathematics discussed earlier called *gematria*, this can be narrowed down to a 4 and 4 relationship, with the removal of the zeroes.

You may be wondering why I am writing about this Hebrew revelation called gematria now. It is because the writers of the Old and New Testaments were Jewish, from the loins of Abraham and the chosen tree of his descendants. This ancient but potent art of mathematics makes the Scriptures come alive and mean so much more. It was not a prejudiced selection; it was a covenant selection.

Please consider this: before science was studied by the human race, we simply discovered how accurate and discerning the mind of

---

[37] Gonzalez & Richards, 2004
[38] Ibid.

God is through the writers of the Holy Writ. It is estimated that the ancient recordings of Moses, in the first book called Genesis, are less than 3,500 years old, yet the science is so accurate and compatible. This synchronized relationship between the sun and the moon is also present with the Creator and the life of Joseph. This unique accordance was also spoken and spelled out from the lips of Jacob as he spoke spiritually over his sons and their future lineage. Rivaled only by Judah, Joseph's future blessing was by far the most enriched and full of promise, more so than the rest. Recorded in Genesis 49, Jacob's words of blessing for Joseph's generations was as follows:

> Joseph *is* a fruitful bough, A fruitful bough by a well; His branches run over the wall. The archers have bitterly grieved him, Shot *at him* and hated him. But his bow remained in strength, And the arms of his hands were made strong By the hands of the Mighty *God* of Jacob (From there *is* the Shepherd, the Stone of Israel), By the God of your father who will help you, And by the Almighty who will bless you *With* blessings of heaven above, Blessings of the deep that lies beneath, Blessings of the breasts and of the womb. The blessings of your father have excelled the blessings of my ancestors, Up to the utmost bound of the everlasting hills. They shall be on the head of Joseph, and on the crown of the head of him who was separate from his brothers. (Gen. 49:22–26 NKJV)

Along with the multiplicity of adorations, I want to explain how the sun and the moon are included in the fruitfulness of Joseph's future. In Genesis 49:25 we read, "And by the Almighty who will bless you with the blessings of heaven above." Verse 26 states, "Up to the utmost bound of the everlasting hills. They shall be on the head of Joseph." In order to have this descriptive occurrence, the installation and the cooperation of nature (the "blessings of heaven" mentioned in Genesis 49:25) are pivotal. This blessing is spiritual, as well as physically productive. The words of the prophet are not just cliché; they are intentional and providential. The blessings of Joseph and his lineage are forevermore, not just during his lifetime. The blessings are eternal!

Let's consider the blessings of the great prophet Moses, who spoke this over the tribe of Joseph before his personal death, over two hundred years or so after Joseph's death. Deuteronomy 33:13–17 tells us:

> About Joseph he said: May the LORD bless his land with the precious dew from heaven above and with the deep waters that lie below; with the best the sun brings forth and the finest the moon can yield; with the choicest gifts of the ancient mountains and the fruitfulness of the everlasting hills; with the best gifts of the Earth and its fullness and the favor of him who dwelt in the burning bush. Let all these rest on the head of Joseph, on the brow of the prince among his brothers. In majesty he is like a firstborn bull; his horns are the horns of a wild ox. With them he will gore the nations, even those at the ends of the Earth. Such are the ten thousands of Ephraim; such are the thousands of Manasseh. (Deut. 33:13–17 NIV)

The prophecies are enriched with the love and mercy of God and nature toward this man of excellence. This prophecy was spoken over the descendants of Joseph and his two sons hundreds of years after they were dead and gone. Why? Because the blessings connected to his sufferings went beyond his personal life, down into the skirts of his offspring and future descendants, just like the previous reference of Exodus 20:5–6 goes beyond the curse of disobedience. It speaks volumes concerning the rich and abundant mercies for those who seek to obey the Creator and His chosen way of living. "Showing mercy to thousands of them that love Me and keep (uphold) My commandments" (Ex. 20:6 NKJV). Exponential growth and development are the potential for all who will follow these criteria.

Finally, let us consider what was spoken by Jacob in reference to the fulfillment of what he spoke. He stated to his sons, "Gather yourselves together, that I may tell you that which shall befall you in the last days" (Genesis 49:1 ASV).

As much as we see how these promises have been fulfilled, we can also see how Joseph's descendants fell short and experienced massive destruction with all of Israel. The Hebrew people or Jews have suffered and prospered in almost every society where they have been dispersed or scattered from their homeland. You cannot take away from the eternal blessing of resilience and how that strength has taken hold and spread through the rest of the world where the Jews are welcomed.

The prophet Moses, in accordance with the patriarch Jacob (whose name was changed to Israel), spoke of the eternal providence that will be available to the Jew first and also to the Gentiles (or non-Jews) who submit to the same mercies of the Creator (Rom. 1:16).

There is a time mentioned for the greatest of what was spoken, called *the last days*. I believe these are the last days and times for things to come together and conclude, both for good and for evil. The choices we make will be the destiny we take, whether it's to our advantage or to our own destruction. I believe, as the prophecies have indicated, the influence of Joseph is eternal and still fruitful in these days and times. The second dream has and is coming with time and seasons.

This book is dedicated to the blessings promised to the willing of heart.

CHAPTER 6

LIGHT IT UP!

The last chapter introduced insights into the possibilities of a greater impact of the life of Joseph than perhaps we had previously considered. We merely scratched the surface of the double-four relationship in regard to the sun and moon. Please understand that I am not an astronomy expert. But with an open heart and willingness to understand the deeper mysteries of life, I share what I see, involving the world's bestseller year after year, *the Holy Bible* in all its languages and translations.

Let's begin with some facts we can all agree on, such as the fact that the sun and moon interact in a precise manner; season after season, year after year. Just as the number *four* has universal implications, there is also another numerical correlation hidden in relation to the sun, the moon, and the life of Joseph. With some of the basic principles of gematria, we will strive toward understanding how this world has a divine order and sequence. Yes, we are talking about Joseph as the main character, but the principle of gematria affects all of our lives. Just like breathing or using water, some things are practical but so vitally important.

We know the sun is the greater light and influences so much more than just the earth. But the moon keeps a monthly stopwatch for our amazing synchronized planet in regards to its solar and lunar cycles. This consideration came from Robert of Palatine, Illinois, as he addresses his question to a *Discovery Magazine* contributor.[39]

Psalm 104:19 says, "He made the moon for the seasons." How does the moon affect our seasons? —Robert of Palatine, IL

The response was:

> Dear Robert,
>
> When we hear the word 'seasons', we think of spring, summer, autumn and winter. We know that it is the tilt of the Earth's axis in relation to our orbit around the Sun that causes these four seasons, *not the Moon*. But the word 'season' also means an appointed time. Ancient people knew that the Moon went through one of its cycles every 29½ days. They made each one of these cycles a month in their calendar. This was very important because they had to know when to plant their crops. In the Old Testament, God told His people to make the first day of each month a special day (Numbers 10:10). The person who wrote this psalm was thanking God for creating light givers like the Moon "for signs, and for seasons, for days, and years" (Genesis 1:14).

Thanks to *Discovery Magazine*, we are given much to consider and understand. We can see how the sun is a greater light and is considered a star. We easily can see how the sun, in its size and reflection of light in our solar system, is greater and more essential to life on earth than the moon itself. But the biblical text speaks of both spheres as rulers or governors of the earth's ecology.

"God made two great lights—the larger one to govern the day, and the smaller one to govern the night. He also made the stars" (Gen. 1:16 NLT).

---

[39] http://www.discoverymagazine.com/digger/d97dd/d9703dd.html.

What we see is two (the sun and the moon) working together as one. The two cannot govern alone, or life as we know it would meet its demise. But the sun is so much greater when compared to the moon. There are many stars in our galaxy that are much larger in size and volume than the moon, yet the moon is much more vital than the stars and other planets, in reference to life on earth. The sun is greater, yet some days you will see the moon up in the sky in the morning and the dawning of a day, as well as the sun. The sun goes up (meaning it can be seen) and goes down, but it never governs with the moon at night. The more frequently seen satellite helps the inhabitants of the earth, as it determines the time and monthly cycles. Just like an accurate wristwatch or clock, the moon cycles, along with the sun, are so precise at 29.53 days to each full moon. In light of this, I received greater clarification regarding their relational functionality to each other.

The precise course and timing of creation and the relationship between the sun, the moon, and the earth has already been predetermined, like the precision timing of a Rolex watch. The chart for 2014 has already been laid out. Here is a chart illustrating this precision:

Lunation	New Moon		First Quarter		Full Moon		Third Quarter		Duration
1126	Jan 1	11:14	Jan 8	03:40	Jan 16	04:53	Jan 24	05:19	29d 10h 24m
1127	Jan 30	21:39	Feb 6	19:22	Feb 14	23:53	Feb 22	17:16	29d 10h 21m
1128	Mar 1	08:00	Mar 8	13:27	Mar 16	17:09	Mar 24	01:46	29d 10h 45m
1129	Mar 30	18:45	Apr 7	08:31	Apr 15	07:43	Apr 22	07:52	29d 11h 30m
1130	Apr 29	06:15	May 7	03:15	May 14	19:16	May 21	12:59	29d 12h 26m
1131	May 28	18:40	Jun 5	20:40	Jun 13	04:12	Jun 19	18:39	29d 13h 29m
1132	Jun 27	08:09	Jul 5	11:59	Jul 12	11:25	Jul 19	02:09	29d 14h 33m
1133	Jul 26	22:42	Aug 4	00:50	Aug 10	18:10	Aug 17	12:26	29d 15h 31m
1134	Aug 25	14:13	Sep 2	11:11	Sep 9	01:38	Sep 16	02:05	29d 16h 01m
1135	Sep 24	06:14	Oct 1	19:33	Oct 8	10:51	Oct 15	19:12	29d 15h 43m
1136	Oct 23	21:57	Oct 31	02:49	Nov 6	22:23	Nov 14	15:16	29d 14h 35m
1137	Nov 22	12:33	Nov 29	10:07	Dec 6	12:27	Dec 14	12:52	29d 13h 04m
1138	Dec 22	01:36	Dec 28	18:32					29d 11h 38m

http://www.timeanddate.com/calendar/moonphases.html?year=2014&n=0

Is this the hand of a Designer of supreme intelligence or what? And yes, I forgot to mention that this chart was just the beginning, as the course relationship with the threesome (the sun, moon, and earth) is already known by precise timing in minutes up until 2099! And that's only where the electronics chose to stop. Dare we tell Rolex or Timex that their precision engineering absolutely has nothing to do with the performance of their product?

Just as the sun is the greater light and the moon is the lesser light, we can rephrase the relationship of oneness to refer to them as the *greater one* and the *lesser one*. The relation symbolizes the number *11*, which is the first double-digit number with value in both places. Ten is double digit, but the zero carries no value. One of our many Bible translations records it as such:

> God made the two great lights, the greater one to govern the day, and the lesser one to govern the night; and he made the stars. (Gen. 1:16 NAB).

The number 11 reflects *a lesser 1* and *a greater 1*. The lesser 1 is an original, singular number 1. The greater 1 is a 10. In the same regard, the number 11 is the first number that reflects itself—in the same image. Again, double zeroes (00) have no value and cannot interact.

The second reflective whole number is 22, then 33, and so forth. Can you see that the two 1s in the number 11 reflects their relationship to each other and their unified relationship to the earth? Just like a marriage, as the holy canon records, "And the two become one" (Eph. 5:23 NIV).

Let's go back to the beginning and we will see an amazing truth that will continue to prevail within the contents of this book. Adam was created as one person, before he became two separate human beings by God's hand (Genesis 2:21-23). The Creator formed the woman (Eve) out of the side of the man. Biologically, male and female have twenty-two sets of autosomes (chromosomes of the same function) in each cell, but the 23rd set, called the sex chromosome, determines if the child will be male or female. The sets of autosomes, 1 through 22, are the same in males and females. The last set of chromosomes in the male are XY combination. The sex of the child is male if a single gene (SRY) signals the Y chromosome. If the Y is not signaled by the SRY, then a female is the result. So each person has 46 chromosomes per cell.

> The DNA in the cells of males has an X and a Y chromosome and this XY pair determines their gender. Females, on the other hand, have a pair of identical X chromosomes, which makes all the difference. To make Eve, the Lord God simply needed to extract from Adam's DNA an X-chromosome and combine it with another newly created X chromosome. A few other minor adjustments in the chromosomes also were in order and the result was that truly man and woman shared the same flesh. 1

So what is our pointed observation here? Just like the sun and the moon have a working 4 and 4 relationship similar to a marriage, as it pertains to the earth, we see the same scenario in the creation of mankind. By removing the 23rd sex combination of chromosomes that determines the difference, we see that every person has twenty-two sets of autosomes (2 x 22), which are *forty four* per cell! When male and female marry, they become one as a reproductive unit. What is the difference between the two individuals? The 23rd set, a XX pairing for the female and a XY for the male, determine their biological roles in reproduction. Though the two reflect one another as humans, the man ultimately has the greater role or responsibility in respect to their relationship and with God. I am not writing this to argue over the truth, but in our example, the sun is certainly greater in strength and responsibility of governing, but without the moon, our planet would soon exist as an uninhabitable planet. I know about the debates but that's my side of the conclusion. Instead of the debate, let's focus on the fact that it's the *forty-four* autosomes

(44) that ultimately makes us equal as humans. Hopefully, reading the rest, you will continue to see how we all need the forty four combinations, physically as well as spiritually.

The moon does more than just magnetically provide high and low tides. If the earth tilted another 10 to 20 degrees, the ferocious storms alone would put life on earth on a timetable, like an hourglass. The sun and the moon have a covenant relationship with earth, and there is only one earth in all of its majesty and life supports.[40]

What does this have to do with our subject, Joseph? Well, Joseph was the eleventh son of Jacob, though by emotional attachment, he was Jacob's favorite; Jacob's number-one son. This was not just Jacob's malady; it was the Creator's as well. The dreams revealed not so much God loving Joseph more, but it refers to how God has to choose one person to be "greatest among you" (Matt. 23:11 NKJV). Without such, you don't have leadership, and all mature people should understand that leadership establishes protocol. So, by numeric value and definition, the responsibility fell on Joseph. In addition to His preserving the people of Jacob's lineage, his preservation strategy saved a great portion of humanity around the globe.

Let's take this a step further. When Joseph had the two dreams, the greater dream was the second dream. Jesus spoke this powerful principle several times in the New Testament record: "The last shall be the first," and "the greater will serve the lesser one" (Matt. 20:16 NASB; Luke 22:27 NKJV). The first dream about him and his brothers was about binding sheaves and showed Joseph's future dominion over his brothers. The second dream not only spoke about his dominion or rule over them, but it also emphasized a greater significance by utilizing the sun and the moon, thus symbolizing greater effect and impact universally. The second dream confirmed the first one, but impact of the second is so much greater. So once again, we see a greater one and a lesser one. To further underscore the greater dream,

---

[40] Jakobsen, Hanne. *Sciencenordic.com*. Science Nordic, 12 Jan. 2012. Web. 30 Jan. 2014. http://sciencenordic.com/what-would-we-do-without-moon.

Joseph included his father, Jacob, in the knowledge of the second dream experience.

After the two dreams combined as one, Joseph's destiny totally changed. He ended up betrayed, separated, imprisoned, and made to be a slave. After he was betrayed again by a frantic adulteress, he was placed in prison. Then while in prison, he met two desperate household managers of the pharaoh. Both had dreams on the same night. The dreams had the same base number (3) as days until pharaoh's judgment, but the interpretation and destinies were polarized. The dreams were fulfilled as Joseph predicted. The dream that spoke of the pharaoh's favor was the greater one. The dream of the chief baker's death was obviously the lesser one. The favorable interpretation for the chief butler was not the only factor that made it greater, but that this dream brought Joseph before the pharaoh. The greater dream became the launch pad of this tremendously gifted leader.

We see at this point that the number 11 is special in many fashions. The difference for me regarding this matter is seeing the other side of the number 11, versus my former knowledge of the number at face value. See, most conservative sources and biblical scholars interpreted that the number 11 only represented confusion. Because the number 10 is a very acceptable and workable grouping multiple, it is considered orderly and seen as another number of completion. The number 12 reflects government and orderly fashion.

So with such acceptable reasoning of the numbers 10 and 12, the number 11 seems to represent too much of something or perhaps not enough. But my studies and new insights have strengthened my resolve that the number 11, if it ever means confusion or lacking, also has a flip side of blessing!

Formerly, the number 11 was a mainstay of sincere Bible scholars to reflect on Jesus and the twelve disciples, before Judas Iscariot betrayed him and committed suicide. But let's just reflect on Joseph, and we will get back to Jesus of Nazareth and how this teaching affects the outlook.

As we examine the number 11, considering what has already been mentioned about the sun and the moon, and even marriage, the number 11 cannot reflect or be defined only as a negative connotation. This is what has been revealed to me: the number 11 is also a connector!

Joseph was given the greater and the lesser call, and even if the call was suffering for a season, it brought forth his purpose and fullness of blessing, just like mothers bearing children. I don't have to tell you that the final days of a full-term pregnancy *are not* a blessing. Right, mothers? Cramps and hard labor? Complications along the way? Yes, it's hard, yet mothers keep having babies, sometimes in multiples. Why would they continue to submit to this process, if it's so hard and even life threatening? They continue because the joy of having children, coupled with the fact of bringing a new life into the world to raise and love and nurture to adulthood, is so fulfilling and rich that it can hardly be described.

Reflecting on Judas and the disciples, their process, too, was an eventual blessing. Without Judas, there would be no resurrection, no Easter or Resurrection Sundays. There would be no hope for a promise of a better life, beyond our natural habitat on earth. Faith now has ground for all-time highs! So in the same manner, the brothers betrayed Joseph, but in the end, Joseph saved a countless multitude and preserved the Hebrew lineage.

Joseph's first two dreams connected him with Egypt, while his brothers overreacted with jealousy and disdain. Joseph's interaction with Pharaoh's officers brought him before Pharaoh two years later. That's four dreams! The Almighty used two sets of back-to-back dreams (shared with his family and Pharaoh's officers) to bring Joseph before the throne of Egypt, to interpret Pharaoh's two dreams. This sequence is definitely providential. So the question remains, which of the pharaoh's dreams were greater: the first one or the last one?

I believe it was Pharaoh's last dream that jarred him to the place of unrest and demanding an answer. The second dream was not as horrific—parched cornstalks devouring plump corn stalks, versus the first dream of skinny, malnourished cows devouring fatted livestock—but the second dream underscored the strength and intent of the first. See, without the second affirming dream, the pharaoh could have just rolled over and counted it just for what it was—a nightmare. The lesser dream magnified the first dream; thus, the last became first, or the greater dream.

I don't want to overlook the number 4, as we have already covered the double-4 factors with Joseph and the sun and moon. We see four dreams with the accurate skill of interpretation that brought Joseph before Pharaoh. It's interesting how the biblical record indicates that Joseph was seventeen years old when he left to find his brothers and was sold into slavery. He was thirty years old when he met the pharaoh face-to-face and was exalted like no other in his era, being promoted from slavery to rule with the pharaoh! That is a thirteen year difference.

Many religious believers share my same reverence for Joseph. Just reflect on how the great patriarch Jacob spoke of him in the same destiny fulfillment as the great prophet Moses. Joseph is highly revered and beloved, even by the Egyptians of his day, as well as the pharaoh himself.

But isn't 13 supposed to be an unlucky number? How can 13 be an unlucky number when God purposed and allowed thirteen tribes, including the priestly tribe of the Levites? Jesus, with His twelve disciples, made a total of 13 as well. Again, I am not saying that the numbers 11 and 13, or any others, do not have negative connotations, but what we are observing is God's ability to use something apparently bad and make something good out of it.

Let's take another gigantic step. The number 13 can actually be the number 4 undercover. How is that possible?

It is possible because of the principles of gematria. Let's peel back the layers of this puzzle and discover why and how the number 13 can be counted as 4 in value.

In a traditional fashion, the Jewish scribes counted not just words but letters. Each letter in the Jewish alphabet also has a numerical value. While the English language has twenty-six letters in its alphabet, the Jewish language has twenty-two letters.

Name	Letter	Value
aleph	א	1
bet	ב	2
gimel	ג	3
dalet	ד	4
he	ה	5
vau (waw)	ו	6
zayin	ז	7
cheth	ח	8
tet	ט	9

Name	Letter	Value
yod	י	10
kap	כ	20
lamed	ל	30
mem	מ	40
nun	נ	50
samek	ס	60
ayin	ע	70
pe	פ	80
tsaddi	צ	90

Name	Letter	Value
qoph	ק	100
res	ר	200
s[h]in	ש	300
tau (taw)	ת	400

When reading the Hebrew language, we read right to left. So the number 1 and its symbol are in the far right corner, at the top of the chart. This is similar to how the Roman alphabet also has numerical values, as we have observed in major literary works.

In its simplest form, gematria is adding up the numerical values of a word, phrase, or paragraph of the Hebrew alphabet. But it is not just adding like in mathematics, as there is also reduction but not necessarily subtraction. Gematria has a reduced value process in which one letter may equal 1 while another letter equals 10 and another letter equals 100, yet when the word or phrase is added up, each letter is only equal to 1. Why? The zeroes are dropped. Therefore, from this example, the total is 3, instead of the three-letter combination (1 + 10 + 100), equaling 111. This is what I am referring to in the 4 and 4 (double-4) relationship of the sun and moon. (Reminder: the sun is 400 times larger, yet 400 times farther away from, the earth.) The zeroes were removed, and just the single-digit number is accounted for. So 400 becomes, or converts to, just the single digit 4.

The fourth process in reduction is called *integral reduced value* and occurs when the total numerical value of the word is greater than 9. In that case, the two digits are added to create a single digit. For instance, if a word or phrase has a numeric value of 27, then the final value of the word or phrase is 9, because 2 + 7 = 9. Because 27 is two digits, the two digits are added together for a single-digit answer. If the number is 346, then you would add them together (3 + 4 + 6) and have 13. Because 13 is still two digits, you would then add up 1 and 3, which equals 4, and that is the integral reduced value of the number 346.

A More Definitive Understanding of Gematria[41]

Absolute value, (in Hebrew: *mispar hechrachi*) also known as *normative value*:

Each letter is given the value of its accepted numerical equivalent; *alef* (the first letter) equals 1, *beit* (the second letter) equals 2, and so on. The tenth letter, *yud* is numerically equivalent to 10, and successive letters equal 20, 30, 40, and so on. The letter *kuf* near the end of the alphabet, equals 100; and the last letter, *tav* equals 400.

In this reckoning, the letters *chaf sofiet (final chaf), mem sofiet, nun sofiet, pei sofiet,* and *tzadik sofiet* which are the final forms of the letters *chaf, mem, nun, pei,* and *tzadik,* used when these letters conclude a word, generally

---

[41] Ibid.

are given the same numerical equivalent of the standard form of the letter. However, sometimes the final *chaf* is considered equivalent to 500, the final *mem* to 600, etc.

Following that alternate form of reckoning, the Hebrew alphabet is a complete cycle. The final *tzadik* equals 900, and thus, the *alef* equals both one and one thousand. Indeed, in Hebrew the same spelling is used for the name of the letter *alef*, and *elef*, meaning *one thousand*.

Noting this phenomenon, Rabbi Avraham Abulafia interprets the verse in Deuteronomy 32:30, "How can one pursue one thousand!" to mean: One, the first number, follows after one thousand in a complete and perfect cycle.

Ordinal value (in Hebrew: *mispar siduri*):

Each of the 22 letters is given an equivalent from one to twenty-two. For example, alef equals 1, kaf equals 11, taf equals 22. The final kaf equals 23, and final tzadik equals 27.

Reduced value (in Hebrew: *mispar katan*, modulus 9 in mathematical terminology):

Each letter is reduced to a figure of one digit. For example, in this reckoning, *alef* equals 1, *yud* equals 10, *kuf* equals 100) would all have a numerical value of 1; *beit* equals 2, *kaf* equals 20, and *reish* equals 200 would all have a numerical value of 2, and so on. Thus, the letters have only nine equivalents, rather than twenty-two.

In both the ordinal and reduced reckonings, the five letters whose form changes when they conclude a word are generally equivalent to their value when they appear within a word. However, they are sometimes given an independent value. For example, the ordinal value of the final nun is at times considered 14, and is at times, 25. Similarly, its reduced value is at times 5, and at other times, 7.

Integral reduced value (in Hebrew, *mispar katan mispari*):
In this fourth method, the total numerical value of
a *word* is reduced to one digit. Should the sum of these
numbers exceed 9, the integer values of the total are
repeatedly added to each other to produce a single-digit
figure. The same value will be arrived at, regardless of
whether it is the absolute values, the ordinal values, or the
reduced values that are being counted.

Now we see how 13 (two digits) is reduced to 4 by the integral
reduced value process. Not to get too bogged down with knowing
its entirety, but gematria provided the Jewish culture with excellent
copy preservations of its scrolls and manuscripts of the sacred
writings. The scribes not only recorded the letters and spelled words,
but they were able to count the value of the original manuscript and
diligently, meticulously went over the copied works of the Torah
to ensure the copy of divine truth and order was not damaged
or made erroneous. Ah-ha! That is why ancient manuscripts had
such accuracy when comparing the two thousand year old Dead
Sea Scrolls with modern-day Torahs and Bibles. It was not just the
reliability through observation of exact letters; their method of
knowing the numerical value of the paragraph or text of interest
also had to match. The Jewish scribes were well trained and were
absolutely the best at their craft because for some, it was their life's
work to dedicate themselves to preserving the words of Yahweh.
Thus, the Torah/Bible has the oldest preserved literary writings in
the world!

We now understand that *Yahweh* (English transliteration,
Jehovah) had His hand on Joseph in a seen and unseen manner.
Joseph is a double 4; he met the pharaoh as a result of four major
dreams (I believe Joseph had other dreams and interpretations that
were unrecorded); and then with 13 (years as a slave to the palace)
being converted to a single digit 4 (integral reduced value), we see
how his life was guided providentially.

Under closer observation, one might add that Joseph had six dreams in all, in order to reach the status of a father/vizier/head-steward to the most powerful ruler in his day. This is true, but Joseph never interpreted his own dreams; they were assumed and pondered and even wrongly considered. Four dreams brought him to Pharaoh (his own and pharaoh's officers), and four dreams were interpreted accurately (the officers' and the pharaoh's dreams), giving him the favorable exaltation he received. Even if we calculate Joseph interpreting only the two dreams of the chiefs, he is forgotten for two years (2 x 2) of additional jail time, which equals 4. Any way you look at it, the number 4 is obviously stellar in the man's life. This insertion of multiplication here is not just hype but of extreme importance as we enter our next phase of understanding. It will definitely heighten our revelation of this truth.

If Joseph could speak today, I know he would give the Lord his God all the praise and the honor. How do I know? Just read and reread the story of his life, and you will see not a man without faults, but nevertheless a grateful and humble man who obeyed and held on to his integrity until his change came, and what a change it was!

CHAPTER 7

HOLDING THE KEYS TO A BIRTHRIGHT

A s many wise and experienced men say, "I would rather be lucky than smart." One can have all the potential and preparation to perform at the next level, but if you don't get the right breaks at the right time, you might miss a real opportunity to prosper. As a religious person, I don't adhere to luck but to the Almighty's grace and mercy, and many times secular and religious mind-sets both refer to this same principle.

Consider sports. How many teams are picked in preseason polls to win their conference and possibly play in a championship game but end up short, never making the playoffs? Why? Because of injuries or because the other team behind in the survey polls was not only as good but was mentally ready to take on the challenge of what it takes to win. Sometimes dissension sets in and divides the team, or the coach and staff never quite adjust to the replacement players that have to step in. There could be a multitude of reasons, but the truth remains: you cannot accomplish greatness without the assistance of others.

Mike Murdock of the Wisdom Center in Denton, Texas, makes great reference to this. He alluded that every Moses needs a Joshua, every Elijah needs an Elisha, every Jesus needs a John, every Michael

Jordan needs a Scotty Pippen, and every Bill Gates needs a Steve Ballmer.

Again, it is the *greater one* who needs the *lesser one* to perform at his maximum capacity. And concerning the individuals spoken of, it is not that the other person is better than the so-called lesser one, but they are better off *with* them than *without* them, to serve and administer to their acknowledged leader.

Joseph was the top man, personally anointed by his Creator, and then was endowed and appointed by the pharaoh. In the appointing, Joseph (*Yosef*) had the greater gifting, and that is exactly what is recorded and what the pharaoh expressed:

> "This will be the land's food supply for the seven years of famine that will come over the land of Egypt, so that the land will not perish as a result of the famine." The proposal seemed good both to Pharaoh and to all his officials. Pharaoh said to his officials, "Can we find anyone else like him? The Spirit of God lives in him!" So Pharaoh said to Yosef, "Since God has shown you all this—there is no one as discerning and wise as you—you will be in charge of my household; all my people will be ruled by what you say. Only when I rule from my throne will I be greater than you." (Gen. 41:35–41 *Complete Jewish Bible*)

And so it is. This great man knew how to put away his pride, search for the right man to help him with his problem, and eventually he found the man, whom he acknowledged was probably more gifted than he was. Pharaoh was greater, but he needed the assistance of someone to oversee the job at hand. Dr. Mike Murdock further shares that many times the successful are those who went out and solved other people's problems, either directly, like a doctor, or with a product that solves the need of the consumer.

Joseph did not make it to the top alone. And as much as I hated to read it, and as much as Joseph hated to go through it, he recognized that without his brother's treachery, he would not have reached his position of power. Without the treachery of Potiphar's wife and the apparent merciful heart of Potiphar himself, Joseph would not have made it to the position of being Pharaoh's right-hand man.

Let's reexamine his betrayal by his brothers, and we will see a powerful underlying truth that redeems one brother above another in their tragic deception of Jacob and betrayal of Joseph.

Without a doubt, Joseph's brothers wanted to hurt him badly, even kill him. Their jealousy for the greatly beloved Joseph reached its height, and Joseph's inability to control his arrogance and discern the brothers' attitude became very noticeable. Jealousy and envy stepped in, and bitterness grew worse as the brothers compounded how Jacob's love for Joseph didn't equal what they felt. When Joseph reached his brothers' camp, they had already discussed possibly killing the dreamer. Reuben, the oldest brother, stepped in and suggested that the brothers shouldn't kill him but should instead throw him in a pit in the wilderness without hurting him. Rueben spoke of the pit with the intention of rescuing Joseph sometime later. The brothers threw him into the pit, but after Rueben left the camp, Judah saw the traders caravanning south and suggested that they sell Joseph to gain profit from his demise. "Why kill him and get nothing from it?" (Gen. 37:26–27). His brothers agreed, and they closed the deal with twenty pieces of silver.

You now know the rest of the story. The reason I reminded us of the ugly drama that took place is because Joseph was *almost killed*, but somebody stepped up for him. In reading the rest of the story, we see that Reuben lost ground, even though Judah was as wrong as two left shoes in this treacherous event. In dealing with his father Jacob (especially when the famine started to grip the world), it was Judah who came to the rescue when they needed it the most.

Judah knew he was wrong in concealing the death of his brother Joseph, and he saw what the fake news did to his father all those years. He stuck his neck out and swore to protect Benjamin with his life as they traveled to see the pharaoh in Egypt, as well as redeem Simeon from prison. Jacob absolutely was against sending Benjamin, but Judah convinced his father that they had no choice. And when the hidden and disguised Joseph refused to let Benjamin go, it was Judah who laid it all out and confessed the wrong actions and pleaded over the frailty of his father, Jacob.

In the meantime, Reuben lost the ground of integrity beyond words with his father. He lost the birthright of the nation that should have been preserved for him as the firstborn son. How? He allowed his lust and perhaps mismanaged sympathy to take hold of his heart, and he slept with his father's concubine. The holy record never expounds on Jacob's reaction and the way he handled the situation. But the Scripture states it clearly:

> Now [we come to] the sons of Reuben the firstborn of Israel. For [Reuben] was the eldest, but because he polluted his father's couch [with Bilhah his father's concubine] his birthright was given to the sons of Joseph [favorite] son of Israel; so the genealogy is not to be reckoned according to the birthright. Judah prevailed above his brethren, and from him came the prince and leader [and eventually the Messiah]; yet the birthright was Joseph's. (1 Chron. 5:1–2 AMP).
>
> The oldest son of Israel was Reuben. But since he dishonored his father by sleeping with one of his father's concubines, his birthright was given to the sons of his brother Joseph. For this reason, Reuben is not listed in the genealogical records as the firstborn son. The descendants of Judah became the most powerful tribe and provided a ruler for the nation, but the birthright belonged to Joseph (1 Chron. 5:1–2 NLT).

In *Jamieson, Fausset & Brown's Commentary on the Whole Bible*, Jamieson explains this violation. He records the reference from Genesis 49:3–4 and states: "Reuben forfeited by his crime the rights and honors of primogeniture. His posterity never made any figure; no judge, prophet, nor ruler, sprang from this tribe."[42]

I recorded the verse twice for a greater perspective. This violation caused the failure of Rueben's plans for his future and his influence in the nation. Instead of carrying the birthright as the oldest and number one son of Jacob, the total package of what actually happened and the fulfillment of Joseph's dreams of coming to power caused Jacob to make the obvious choice. But you will also see that Judah's intervention in a soldier-like manner of sacrifice bought him favor. He now was promised a future leader who would come out of his own lineage.

The birthright is further explained in the *Holman Bible Dictionary*:

> Esau forfeited his birthright to his brother Jacob for the sake of a meal of lentil stew and bread (Genesis 25:29–34). The birthright consisted of the special privileges that belonged to the firstborn male child in a family. Prominent among those privileges was a double portion of the estate as an inheritance. If a man had two sons, his estate would be divided into three portions, and the older son would receive two. If there were three sons, the estate would be divided into four portions, and the oldest son would receive two. The oldest son also normally received the father's major blessing. Indeed, the Hebrew word for blessing (berakah) is virtually an anagram of the word that means both birthright and firstborn (bekorah). Legal continuation of the family line may also have been included among the privileges of the firstborn son. Deuteronomy 21:15–17 prohibited a father from playing favorites among his sons by trying to give the birthright to other than the firstborn.[43]

---

[42] Fausset, et.al., 1999
[43] Butler, 1991.

Remember that earlier I stated that Jacob's descriptive blessing of Joseph's future was only rivaled by Judah's prophetic future. Here is what was stated concerning Judah, out of Jacob's mouth:

Judah, you *are he* whom your brothers shall praise; Your hand *shall be* on the neck of your enemies; Your father's children shall bow down before you. Judah *is* a lion's whelp; From the prey, my son, you have gone up. He bows down, he lies down as a lion; And as a lion, who shall rouse him? The scepter shall not depart from Judah, Nor a lawgiver from between his feet, Until Shiloh comes; And to Him *shall be* the obedience of the people (Gen. 49:8–10 NKJV).

Judah was now blessed and exalted among his brethren, even though the birthright still belonged to Joseph. Prophetically, he received the promise of Shiloh, the coming worldwide ruler among Jews and Gentiles alike. As stated previously, you can be blessed or gifted with all the potential in the world, but if someone does not undergird and support your broad base, you will struggle and most likely not reach your full capacity of service and ability. Joseph was blessed, but Judah stepped up and matured in character and status as he learned his lessons. Judah was not a perfect man, and he suffered through his mistakes and grew to be a champion. As such, his lineage took on his likeness and became the strongest military tribe among the house of Israel.

What were Judah's mistakes? Let's list a few.

1. Judah had three sons, and the first two died early. The third was supposed to married the same woman (a Jewish custom of honoring a lost loved one).
2. The Torah records that the first son was wicked, and the second son proved he was disrespectful to his father's wishes and did not want to honor his older brother. These two boys took on some of the character traits of Judah.

3. Then Judah, fearful of his third son marrying this woman with a bad omen (blameshifting—none of it was her fault), never brought him back after he became of age, and thus he broke his promise.

4. His wife died, and while on the journey to do his trading business, he chose to lay overnight with an apparent prostitute. The woman wasn't a prostitute, but was his neglected daughter-in-law, and she got pregnant. Once he found out about it, he called her in for impending judgment. She gave some of Judah's belongings to one of Judah's assistants with the message, "I am pregnant by the man who owns these" (Gen. 38:25 NIV). Judah dropped his head and admitted his guilt. The lady had twins, and he never engaged with her again sexually.

5. And then, of course, Judah sold his brother to the Midianite traders.

You see, Judah was problematic and troubled for quite some time, but he grew up and redeemed both the time and himself. This shows you how gracious God in heaven can be to the heart that is willing to make a change. Hopefully you will find encouragement in this, realizing that once you have messed up, you can get up, learn from your mistakes, repent, and do it no more. Get out of the bad lifestyle, and get it moving in the right direction. Like Judah, God may not be through with your original destiny of mercy and blessing. You have to make the sacrifice: you can't have it both ways!

I would like to expound on a few more insights into the Hebrew birthright. First Chronicles 5:1–2 says so much more, but it is found in the definition of the word. Just as the Hebrew meaning for *birthright* is intertwined with *firstborn*, it is not an accident that the word *blessing* comes from the same root. Our compound words produce the same effect in the English language; the two meanings and values sometimes go beyond the two being combined. It sometimes increases the volume beyond the combination, into multiples.

That is what I see in 1 Chronicles 5. The birthright blessing of inheritance on Reuben was split, and the greater blessings fell on Joseph and his sons. But 1 Chronicles 5:2 further states that Judah prevailed, and in his prevailing, he received the promise that the Messiah or Shiloh would come through his lineage. Let's consider this double-strength combination.

Remember how we elaborated on the importance of the number 4 and the number 11? Well, Judah was the fourth-born son to Jacob, whose corrupted wisdom helped preserve his brother's life, and then after his mediatory work with the hidden, or yet-to-be-identified, Joseph, it was proven that he was willing to sacrifice it all. The name *Judah* means *praise*.[44] Praise given to anyone who is worthy of it serves as a multiplying force to encourage the person to keep on doing what they are doing. Yes, the Lord was with Joseph on every side, but the Almighty uses people as vessels of his goodness to others. Humanly speaking, Judah served as Joseph's savior (from the clutches of his brethren), and this is exactly what was promised to Judah prophetically.

We see clearly that Judah was the fourth son who received word of the most promising of all events, the coming Messiah, along with Joseph, who received eternal blessings as ancient as the hills and mountains.

I believe wholeheartedly that Joseph is a mathematical equation and a product of the heavens. His dreams indicate and compound the same conclusion. He was the eleventh born of the fourth wife to have baby. Once again, we see 11 x 4 = 44. In light of gematria (digit counting), the numeral 44 is looked upon and can be considered as a double 4. Both Joseph and Judah were generational leaders with generational blessings, as a combined force of goodness and power. We have spoken about Joseph being a double 4, already. Joseph's multiple of identification is the number 44. Do you see it? Here's further confirmation of this truth. Joseph was exalted at the age of thirty and was forty-four years old, after the seven good years and the seven deadly years of drought. By the time Joseph was forty-four

---

[44] http://dictionary.reference.com/browse/judah.

years old, the trial and tribulation that threatened the known world was over, and restorative weather patterns thereafter occurred.

What is unique about a generational equation? A generational equation is not just addition; it is multiplication. Generations are multiples of a lineage. It is not singular; it is now ranks or sets of order. The number of children each child has determines how large the family will be.

This principle of multiplying is what I will be referring to as *the Joseph Principle*. A principle is a general law or truth that works anywhere it is applied. It was in studying Joseph's life and how his destiny was connected to his dreams that I began to see this multiple.

For further confirmation of this dynamic truth, we have another prophet who sees this working principle come to pass. Just like the compound word *birthright,* which has the connotation of increase and fruitfulness, the prophet Ezekiel records some prophetic words that have already been fulfilled, yet still are to come to fullness.

> The word of the LORD came to me: "Son of man, take a stick of wood and write on it, 'Belonging to Judah and the Israelites associated with him.' Then take another stick of wood, and write on it, 'Belonging to Joseph (that is, to Ephraim) and all the Israelites associated with him.' Join them together into one stick so that they will become one in your hand. "When your people ask you, 'Won't you tell us what you mean by this?' Say to them, 'This is what the Sovereign LORD says: I am going to take the stick of Joseph—which is in Ephraim's hand—and of the Israelite tribes associated with him, and join it to Judah's stick. I will make them into a single stick of wood, and they will become one in my hand.'" (Ezek. 37:15–19 NIV)

The event is the prediction that the tribal split of the nation of Israel will be healed or mended. Joseph, or *the stick of Ephraim*, represents the northern tribes that broke away from the southern remnants of

Judah and Benjamin, with representation of loyalists from the other tribes after the rule of Solomon. Once again, the influence of Joseph through his sons is predominant; and therefore, the prophets referred to the ten breakaway tribes as Joseph, or Ephraim, which became the largest tribe of the nine others, including his brother, Manasseh.

Ezekiel is recording this about 1,200 years after the life of Joseph and giving credence to the prophecy of Jacob over Joseph's sons.[45] The prophet predicts that the tribes of the north (Joseph) will eventually become one again, with the south (Judah) as a nation. Did this come to pass?

Yes it did! After Hitler's genocide attempt in World War II, the rebirth of the nation of Israel became a modern-day miracle in May 1948.[46] After tremendous suffering and six million dead in less than four years, the United Nations voted to approve and recognize Israel as a state/nation once again. But not before they paid a great price. The suffering was immense, and they still had to fight wars and attacks by neighboring countries afterward. Yet the prophecy prevailed, and it seems like a divine hand of mercy was involved. Just like the prophecy stated, Israel is no longer recognized as a divided nation, and they have one government via the Knesset.[47]

It is easy to look back on things and think the split was no big deal. But this split of the north and the south is well documented in history, as well as in the holy canon. The split occurred under the reign of King Jeroboam, and the ten-tribe union established their own government with their own kings, their own commerce, their own religious affairs, and so forth. They fought battles against one another, as well as tried to be allies in the time of war against foreign powers. Only captivities and sufferings by foreign nations brought them back together.

Once again, we see two becoming one. This adjoining is not just side-by-side and additional. This is a prediction of intertwining and

---

[45] http://bibleencyclopedia.com/ezekiel.htm.
[46] http://www.adolfhitler.dk/index.htm.
[47] http://www.jewishvirtuallibrary.org/jsource/Politics/how_govt_works.html.

blending. The result is much fruitfulness. This is a cross-sectioning, like an intersection of two major roads or highways. In agricultural terms, this union prediction will produce cross-breeding, like a hybrid seed that eventually bears hybrid fruit, with a new taste.

So what are we actually observing here? In reference to this newly identified Joseph Principle, Joseph has already been equated as a symbolic forty four or a double 4. But as a prophetic stick, he is the 11th son (the northern tribes), being reunified with Judah, the 4th son of Jacob (the southern tribes) to re-create as a new nation. This 44 factor is predicted to usher in "The son of David", if you read the rest of Ezekiel 37. This is not 11 plus 4; but it is a multiple of 11 times 4, with a greater re-enforcement of fruitfulness. This 44 factor was equipped in the life of Joseph, who was the precursor of the promised Messiah or Shiloh. He had all the qualities of the messiah and was respected by all. He was a Hebrew who served in a Gentile world; he was brought to power and held authority over all he dealt with. The whole world needed him for a season, and many traveled night and day to see Him for their life's sustenance. Here is one of many Messianic passages that predicted such a person:

> For unto us a Child is born, Unto us a Son is given; And the government will be upon His shoulder. And His name will be called Wonderful, Counselor, Mighty God, Everlasting Father, Prince of Peace. Of the increase of *His* government and peace *There will be* no end, Upon the throne of David and over His kingdom, To order it and establish it with judgment and justice From that time forward, even forever. The zeal of the LORD of hosts will perform this. (Isa. 9:6–7 NKJV)
>
> So, what is next for Israel? The latter verses of Ezekiel 37:22–25 say that this is a prelude (the rebirthing of the nation) to a greater king than David entitled, "the mighty God."

Isaiah 9:6–7 was not talking about Joseph. Joseph was the greatest example of such and is a precursor sign of the prophecy. Joseph was a prototype of Judah's prophecy of Shiloh's coming. Isaiah lived about one thousand years after Joseph. But Jews and Gentiles alike look forward to a greater day with a leader endowed with like qualities; this is nothing short of what the prophecy states, from the lips of Jacob, to Judah, and by the pen of Moses.

As we end this chapter and our meditations of the prophecy of Ezekiel 37, please consider this as well. The two sticks, that symbolically represented Joseph as the northern tribes, and Judah, the southern division of the divided nation of Israel, are mentioned as being put side by side to make them one. These sticks were symbolically bound together, which is a sign of two becoming one. It is the language and understanding of a true covenant. If you can see this, it is two equal sticks standing up against the other, which provides the picture of the number eleven (11)! This unique display underscores why the number 11 can no longer be looked upon as confusion and chaos only. We must begin to see it as a divine connection to the next phase of God's intent. This union will usher in what is written above. The coming of Shiloh!

CHAPTER 8

THE JOSEPH PRINCIPLE

Joseph has been gone for about 3,800 years, yet his legacy still compels us. By opening our hearts and minds, we can better absorb the message that God, Yahweh, our Creator, has sent us through Joseph's incredulous life. His message has deeply touched me, and I believe that—if you suspend disbelief long enough to explore this exciting message—it will deeply touch you, as well. Faith from the heart is required in any miracle. Open yourself to the miraculous. *Believe!*

> And without trusting, it is impossible to be well pleasing to
> God, because whoever approaches him must trust that he
> does exist and that he becomes a Rewarder to those who
> seek him out. (Heb. 11:6 *Complete Jewish Bible*)

We must *trust beyond what we can see and feel!* If we trust Him, we experience true freedom in a world beyond belief. Joseph had this kind of faith, and look where it led him! Unfortunately, there are many nonbelievers and some 'too highly educated' for their own good who simply refuse to believe, and they are missing the fun! Joseph is not the only one who had dream indicators that came to fruition. He is not the only one who has experienced *déjà vu*—that sense of having been in a place or situation before actually arriving.

Unbelievers are people who simply don't pay attention. Proof is all around you! If you don't believe, just ask for proof. That's right! Ask God if He really exists, to make Himself personally known to you. Ask God to help you believe and know truth. Then try not to be surprised or overwhelmed when things happen in a manner that may be only you are in tune. In my experience, I find Him to be very personal and detailed to my various needs of affirmation.

The Joseph Principle shows us how the Creator endowed Joseph with such consistent integrity that the presence of God remained with him at all times. Everything Joseph was involved with increased. When he ran the household of Potiphar, the household ran smoothly, despite the language barrier. When he took care of trading and buying goods, finances grew and prospered. If anyone needed advice, Joseph's perceptions were acute and his suggestions wise to the task at hand. If the prison population was unjust, he knew how to handle the struggle and create an agreeable atmosphere. He not only knew how to serve his masters, but he also knew how to work fairly with commoners and other slaves. He just knew how to make the best out of a bad situation because what he had was greater than his environment. He possessed the Blesser as well as the blessing!

This is the key that we can (and need to) mimic; Joseph never injured or went against whatever was put upon him. He remained respectful to what he sensed as a child. The third to the fourth generation of a true man of integrity who fears God has the keys to explode! He has the keys to expand, to see increase, and to prosper. I shared the 44 factor in prior chapters, and Joseph personified this 44 factor (the Joseph Principle). Now we, too, can have our due portion. How? *We must believe!*

Let's explore a major foundation of the Law of Moses, which provides further instruction in how we can strengthen our belief and thus prosper through this incredible Joseph Principle.

> Hear, O Israel: The Lord our God, the Lord *is* one! You
> shall love the Lord your God with all your heart, with all

your soul, and with all your strength. And these words
which I command you today shall be in your heart. (Deut.
6:3-6 NKJV)

Did you recognize it? It's the 44 factor! Let me explain how the
Joseph Principle is illustrated in these verses.

The Lord our God, also called *Adoni,* Lord of all, is *our Lord.*
When we believe that He is *our Lord,* we see that He is *the greater
one,* and we are *the lesser ones.* There it is, again—the number 11. We
covered earlier that the number 11 is a covenant number, that it is a
marriage. When two are married and walk together in oneness, they
look like walking 11s!

The text states that the Lord God (the greater one) dwells in an
ongoing relationship as *one*; we are unified or together. Symbolically,
as well as in spirit, the number 11 is illustrated perfectly here.

Now let's review what the verse above says about loving the Lord
through three distinct areas:

1. Your heart
2. Your soul
3. Your strength (or might)

Jesus of Nazareth was considered a master teacher among the
common people. He expressed it like this in the Roman culture using
common Greek language.

Jesus said to him, "You shall love the Lord your God
with all your heart, with all your soul, and with all your
mind." This is the first and great commandment. And the
second is like it: "You shall love your neighbor as yourself."
On these two commandments hang all the Law and the
Prophets. (Matt. 22:37-40 NKJV)

Jesus reminded His audience to fulfill *what is written*! To love God in oneness, with all your heart, with all your soul, and with all your mind. One moment, you say. What happened to *all your might?* The *all* is your strength or might. The *all* is everything you possess in strength and energy. So Jesus was sharing with us that we must love God with:

1. Our hearts (inward motivations)
2. Our souls (imaginations)
3. Our minds (intellect)
4. Our all or might (strength or energy)

The soul suggests one's thoughts, will, and emotions. Jesus was describing a deeper truth about the soul-realm of an individual. Your heart is the central control of your spiritual being or your spiritual self. As it has been stated, "We do not think words, we see pictures and use words to describe, what we see, or imagine."[48] Another Scripture in the New Testament of the holy canon reveals that Jesus did not come to destroy the law but to fulfill it (Matt. 5:17–18). Jesus simply added not new knowledge but hidden knowledge concerning one's being.

Just in case the readers might think I stretched this truth beyond the norm, another reference to the Shema is reflected in Luke 10.

> So he answered and said, 'You shall love the Lord your God with all your heart, with all your soul, with all your strength, and with all your mind,' and 'your neighbor as yourself.'" (Luke 10:27 NKJV)

From this reference, we can see the four compartments of mankind more clearly, as well as the relationship mankind needs to

---

[48] Mishlove, Jeffery, Dr., prod. "Thinking Allowed Conversations on the Leading Edge of Knowledge and Discovery." *Language and Consciousness- Part 1: Are Our Thoughts Constrained by Language?* Web. 05 Jan. 2014. Transcript-Interview with author, Steve Pinker, Ph.D.

display with one another. Shall we go a step further? The greater one is oneself, and your neighbor is the lesser one. No love and respect for self leaves one empty and void to love, respect, and honor other human beings on a consistent basis.

This is your number 4 factor and the hybrid relationship of you and your God. These four parts of your being gives you the numeric formula 11 x 4 = 44. The 44 factor in one's life will produce an overflow or ability to prosper when God and man come together. Like the number 11, mankind is your reflection. *The Joseph Principle is available to you!* This grace multiplied comes by the increase of these areas of knowledge and worship; the giving of oneself in fullness of loving God Himself. These words are recorded about Jesus of Nazareth in Luke:

> And Jesus increased in wisdom and stature, and in favour
> with God and man. (Luke 2:52 KJV)

The favor of God in this text aligns itself with grace, blessings, increase, good fortune, and the goodness of the Almighty. This description of the humanity of Jesus was the same spirit of well-being that was on Joseph of Egypt.

We now know that the number 4 is connected to awareness—universally, globally and earthly. A double 4, like 44 (of the two 4s, one is greater than the other, but one whole number), takes universal awareness to a whole new level. Joseph was not just in the world and aware of his environment; he was given dreams that dictated that he would become someone special in the world. In other words, the 44 factor goes beyond Joseph and beyond the Old Testament saints. The Joseph Principle always was, is now, and always will be with us. Like the prophecies about Joseph, this principle is universal as well as eternal.

Here are some examples in the Old and New Testament of the Joseph Principle of multiplication. And yes, Jesus operated in it, but you would have never known it without *the keeping of the law.* Obedience is a major part, but let's remember the scribes and how they preserved the law. The other side of keeping the law was how they actually kept the truth from being spoiled or injured or made erroneous—how? Through gematria! Jesus of Nazareth came to fulfill the law. The way the scribes kept or preserved the law, Jesus actually practiced in spirit and truth.

Let's begin with two people who made up one of the greatest tandems of world-class ministry, a prophet and his protégé, Elijah and Elisha. Right off the bat, we see the number 11, as Elijah is the master prophet and Elisha was his disciple/servant (the greater one and the lesser one). But they met after Elijah faced discouragement and depression from dealing with the likes of Ahab and his wicked wife, Jezebel. God healed Elijah's heart by interacting with His mighty servant. Elijah went to a cave where Moses used to reside on Mt. Sinai, or Horeb, and the Lord met him there by voice and natural phenomenon (1 Kings 19:11–12). God showed his presence to Elijah in four ways:

1. A strong wind
2. A fire
3. An earthquake
4. And a still, small voice

We shared that the number 44 also refers to a messianic connotation or reference. *Messiah* means *the anointed one.* The Messiah is the one who has been chosen and touched by the Most High. Elijah was already well aware of who was there with him. He knew it was the Lord God Himself! There is the number 11 again— the greater 1 and the lesser 1. God was renewing Elijah's strength and measuring his willingness to believe again. Using four ways of refreshment, He was renewing Elijah's mojo: the 44 factor. God then spoke to Elijah, giving him four more instructions to remain in office, including meeting Elisha. He told Elijah to go and:

1. anoint a new king of Syria;
2. anoint a new king of Israel;

3. meet Elisha, his protégé and future replacement; and
4. make his way back to Damascus because he still had an ongoing responsibility to God, to himself (fulfillment and purpose), and to others.

(1 Kings 19:15–16)

When Elijah meets Elisha, Elisha immediately responds to the call by butchering his yoke of oxen, having a meal, and saying last good-byes before leaving. He was plowing with twelve yokes of oxen and managing his father's farm, with other plowmen as servants. In other words, Elisha subtracted one set of oxen, his own personal plow, and left eleven yoke of oxen for his father's farming. We see once again four (instructions) and a master, Elijah (the greater one), calling his new disciple/servant, Elisha (the lesser one), and we have the eleven yokes left (a double confirmation). The sum total still can be equated as 4 x 11 = 44, or *the Joseph Principle* of multiplied grace.

Let me share my conviction, and I hope you will see the point I am trying make. I am not manipulating the numbers in these biblical examples. Elisha could have owned seven yokes, fourteen yokes, or any other number. The Lord God could have given Elijah two, three, or six instructions. I am just communicating the textual layout and providing truthful insight because I believe the text speaks for itself the knowledge that God wants us to observe. Some might say, "Okay, I see the numbers, but what's all this multiplying to figure out what God is or is not doing?" That's a good question! As mankind, we question the truth all the time. We say, "Hold on, I have to figure this out."

I remember when I was in middle school in my small town of Coatesville, and our math teacher separated the class into smaller groups of four or five students and gave each group a math problem to figure out. My small group got along extremely well; we were funny and quirky, we sang as we studied, and we even named our group. We were the Coatesville Calculators! In our group were two young Jewish boys (who I like to think of as my personal Elijah and Elisha), along with my best friend, Bruce. Though I chuckle when I think about our humorous disposition, I also must humble myself before God, realizing He was orchestrating my steps even way back then (six months after my mother's death)—using that time to stir my imaginative and creative mind mathematically to see what others sometimes miss.

God multiplies and calculates too. Nothing mankind does is original. Genesis 1 reminds us that Yahweh made us "in our image, after our likeness," in reference to Himself (Gen. 1:26 KJV). Multiplying and figuring out stuff is a great part of life. If we are not haphazard and if we like things orderly, why wouldn't God the Creator also do things in like fashion, just as when man was first created? This truth is actually recorded in Job.

> God understands its way, And He knows its place For He looks to the ends of the Earth, *And* sees under the whole heavens [4], To establish a weight for the wind, and apportion the waters by measure. When He made a law for the rain, And a path for the thunderbolt [4], Then He saw *wisdom* and declared it; He prepared it, indeed, He searched it out [4]. And to man He said, "Behold, the fear of the Lord, that *is* wisdom, and to depart from evil *is* understanding." (Job 28:23–28 NKJV, numerals in brackets above added by the author).

Please notice my references to the number 4 in the verses above. The number 4 alludes to *the world, world related, universal, and earthly*, right? So look how Job, who has a prophetic gift, records the mind and actions of the Creator. The writer declares that the Creator calculates and figures things out before He moves. From creation to the creative, He controls ongoing events of nature itself. What's illustrated here?

1. Wisdom management of the earth (vv.23–24)
2. The strategy of the ecology (vv.25–26)

3. The wisdom of earthly creation (v.27)
4. The way to true wisdom

Without delving into unnecessary depths, we see four factors in each verse combination. Why? Because the Lord God is revealing His way of calculating things as the all-knowing God that He is in communicating about Himself to Job. I did not write these verses; I am just delivering them. God wants you to know that you are not alone, and you cannot do this by yourself. He created it and allowed it, and this is how He operates. If you give God the respect He is due, He will show you more.

The book *Numbers in Scripture* by E. W. Bullinger lists facts of nature and productivity.[49] This list shares how consistent the number 7 comes up, as it relates to gestation—an animal or mammal being developed in the womb until birth. Insects are also mentioned.

> The various periods of gestation also are commonly a multiple of seven, either of days or weeks.
>
> With insects, the ova are hatched from seven half-days (as the wasp, bee, etc.); while with others it is seven whole days. The majority of insects require from 14 (2 x 7) to 42 (6 x 7) days; the same applies to the larva state.
>
> With Animals the period of gestation of:
> The mouse is 21 (3 x 7) days
> The hare and rat, 28 (4 x 7) days
> The cat, 56 (8 x 7) days
> The dog, 63 (9 x 7) days
> The lion, 98 (14 x 7) days
> The sheep, 147 (21 x 7) days

---

[49]   Bullinger, 2005.

With Birds, the gestation of:
The common hen is 21 (3 x 7) days
The duck, 42 (6 x 7) days

With the Human species it is 280 days (or 40 x 7).[50]

God is simply awesome and excellent beyond words! How can anyone rightfully believe that this numerical sequence occurred in nature, without believing in God's omniscience (all-knowing power)? This is only one minute example of God's design and order of living things in the universe. I encourage readers to pick up Bullinger's book to consider the facts.

Let's further address the point: Does God calculate before things happen or before a judgment or decision is made? When the nation of Israel was being disobedient to the law of letting the land rest every seventh year and fell prey to idolatry (Lev. 25), the Lord sent judgment through the nation of Babylon.

What was the total number of years of their bondage and captivity? Seventy years under the heavy hand of the Babylonians. Why seventy? Because they violated seventy sabbatical years of letting the land rest from agricultural labor every seventh year. Without debate, the land rested during their probationary period!

There is also the familiar story in Numbers 14, where the children of Israel balked at God's command to go into the Promise Land. They chose unbelief and suffered an extended time of unproductivity in the wilderness. Moses sent twelve spies into the land for a report that confirmed that the land was excellent for grazing and agriculture. The size of the fruit there was phenomenal. The spies returned with a good report of the physical fruitfulness of the land, but they were terrified of their surrounding neighbors, who were much bigger and stronger in size. For that reason, they refused to move.

---

[50] Ibid.

Two spies, Caleb and Joshua, stood up and said, "If God said it; it is done" (Num. 14:24, 30, 38). The nation was persuaded by the unbelief and fear of the ten spies, and the anger of Jehovah was kindled. He revealed His judgment through Moses. "This generation of adults, twenty and over, shall not enter the Promise Land. You will remain in this wilderness for forty long years, until all of you are gone [dead]" (Num. 14:28–34).

Why forty years? Because ten of the twelve spies led the rebellion of fear not to enter in, and it was now the tenth time the people rebelled against His evident power since Israel had left Egypt and crossed the Red Sea, using signs and wonders. Add this to the fact that the spies were commissioned for forty days—the number of trials and testing. Each day of their commission, which ended in total disobedience, was judged as one year. At the end of the nation's tenth rebellion, led by ten spies of eldership under Moses, the God of Abraham, Isaac, and Jacob had had enough! The only possible turnaround for a second chance was the next generation.

We see here a caring God who wants the best for His people, but He requires their trust. He showed them what He was able to do, yet they refused to follow through. God calculates in the courts of heaven, and He determines judgment. He calculated their steps, how many times they disobeyed, how many people were involved, and what must be done. This is how justice works. Many parents understand that there are guidelines and restrictions in governing a household. Many times your child will try your patience, but you must lead him or her in the right direction. That's not mean; that's love in action.

Let's now look at the ministry of Jesus of Nazareth and the New Testament commentary of His ministry among men, as seen through the lens of gematria.

At the pool of Bethesda, it is recorded that there were sick and afflicted people of every kind (John 5). Now let us consider the elements of gematria that appear in the text. Out of the multitude of diseases that were present, only four conditions or categories are listed in John 5:3:

1. Impotence
2. Blindness
3. Halted
4. Withered

The featured healing miracle that took place happened to a man who was sick for thirty-eight years. Again, we look at the fact of two digits, 3 and 8. When we add these two together, we see 3 + 8 = 11.

Now we have four groups representing various conditions of poor health, and then we have the healing miracle of the man who was sick for thirty-eight years. This man could not walk at all, but after the miracle he was suddenly walking. According to the Joseph Principle, we see 4 x 11 = 44. Then Jesus went against the grain of the sabbatical law and perspective of the religious leaders. Jesus broke the law by working on the Sabbath! The Sabbath was also referenced as the eternal day in light of God creating everything in six days, and He rested on the seventh day (Gen. 2:2–3). The seventh day represents the hope and promise of eternal peace—one day with the coming Messiah. Joseph was Jacob's son given the most definite prophecies of eternal blessings, along with Judah having an eternal Messiah in his lineage.

Let's look at another example of how this unique principle was upheld at the end of Jesus' earthly life and ministry. Jesus was already crucified and died, and then He resurrected, according to the prophets and the New Testament writers. Instead of handpicking a new twelfth disciple after Judas Iscariot betrayed Christ and hung himself, Jesus remained with only the eleven.

When you consider the thoroughness of his leadership and administration, this seems kind of strange and incomplete. Yet when we apply the new knowledge we have uncovered together, including the additional insight concerning the number 11, our understanding has to expand pass a disorganized conclusion; to consider that the Resurrected One did not shore up this foundation of twelve original disciples for a divine purpose. If He had no problem with it, then we have to trust His wisdom accordingly. By doing so, something else unfolds and is revealed.

Jesus left His disciples with instructions concerning their earthly calling and mission. In the gospels of Matthew and Mark, we see affirmation of the fact that Jesus instructed His followers to spread this good news of His message and resurrection, in and throughout the world (Matt. 28:19–20; Mark 16:15). But in the first chapter of the book of Acts, Jesus shares how to spread this message strategically. This is what scholars and teachers have entitled the Great Commission. Jesus instructs us to first share the news at home, then further the plan of outreach:

> But you shall receive the power of the Holy Ghost coming upon you, and you shall be witnesses unto me in Jerusalem, and in all Judea, and Samaria, and even to the uttermost part of the Earth. (Acts 1:8 *Douay-Rheims 1899 American Edition*)
> 1. Jerusalem was home.
> 2. Judea was the next place of ministry.
> 3. Samaria is the next region.
> 4. Finally, we witness to the uttermost parts of the world.

As clearly identified above, this represents four strategic areas of outreach.

The Joseph Principle is quickly observed as Jesus' eleven core disciples (absent the betrayer, who was not replaced immediately) were given such vital instructions to carry out before the resurrected Jesus ascended back to His former glory. We see the same scenario: $11 \times 4 = 44$.

What was accomplished when Joseph was forty-four years old? The deathly famine was completed. The famine that was killing men and women and threatening everybody's livelihood was now over. When Jesus gave up his life, He said on the cross, "It is finished" (John 19:30 KJV). He further shared how He came to finish the work of His Father and now it was completed. He basically stated, "Because of my obedience to the Father, your faith in My completed work will lead you from death into life everlasting."

Did you notice it? The fourth place is a reference to *the uttermost parts of the world*. This is verified truth.

Here is my affirming word:

> But if he will not hear, take with you one or two more, that 'by the mouth of two or three witnesses every word may be established. (Matt. 18:16 NKJV)

> For precept *must be* upon precept, precept upon precept, line upon line, line upon line, Here a little, there a little. (Isa. 28:10 NKJV)

> [*Coming with Authority*] This *will be* the third *time* I am coming to you. "By the mouth of two or three witnesses every word shall be established." (2 Cor. 13:1 NKJV)

The forty or so persons/authors that the Lord God used to formulate our present-day holy canon (the sixty-six books) were not man's work alone. It was the Almighty's work, through men. Over the 1,500 years in which the Holy Bible was compiled, the men who wrote it came from every stratus of society, most having never met one another, having lived in different regions and being of various ages. Yet their words and thoughts never break the spirit of truth, if one is humble enough and discerning enough to listen and be trained.

I intentionally saved this example—the one I believe is the best— for last, as I know many are believers but not *receivers* from the likes of this unknown author (me) up to this point.

Let's consider the longing of the Jews, who were under the tyrannical Roman government, still awaiting the promises of a coming Messiah through the lines of Judah and the household of King David. They believed in a coming deliverer, in the power of Moses, yet were under the authority of the pharaohs and the Caesars. Their faith hinged on deliverance from the Romans, just as Moses provided deliverance of the children of Israel about 1,400 years earlier. When the children of Israel left Egypt, it is recorded that there were 600,000 men alone, not including women and children (Ex. 12:37). It is believed that at least 2 to 3 million came out of Egypt during this time. This desired expectation comes out when Jesus of Nazareth goes into a mountain next to the sea of Tiberius, which was also called the Sea of Galilee. The feast of the Passover was near, which commemorates the Jews' dramatic escape from Egyptian bondage. This is a constant story of reference, from the prophets to the Psalms of David and writers, that their God is true and benevolent in the lives of His people.

Jesus asked His disciples where they could find enough bread and food to feed the multitudes. The disciples were incredulous, saying something along the lines of, *"You must be kidding, Lord!"* Andrew commented that there was a boy who had five barley loaves and two small fishes. Jesus directed everyone to sit down. The number of men alone was five thousand. After Jesus gave thanks to His Heavenly Father, He gave loaves of bread to His disciples, with the fish. The Scriptures record the miracle:

> And Jesus took the loaves; and when he had given thanks, he distributed to the disciples, and the disciples to them that were set down; and likewise of the fishes as much as they would. When they were filled, he said unto his disciples, Gather up the fragments that remain, that nothing be lost. Therefore they gathered them together, and filled twelve baskets with the fragments of the five barley loaves, which remained over and above unto them that had eaten. (John 6:11–13 NKJV)

The disciples picked up twelve baskets full of leftovers. Without question Jesus was signifying through this heavenly blessing a message of provision for His twelve disciples. Yes, He was surely speaking to the multitude of Jews, who remained in awe and saw the leftovers in the baskets as a sign that God still could provide for the twelve tribes of Israel.

Now when we consider the Joseph Principle of adding and multiplying, something else is revealed in dynamic fashion.

In multiplying the initial numbers, two fishes and five barley loaves, we get ten. By multiplying, as Jesus did with the fishes and loaves, we consider five thousand men, and 5,000 x 10 = 50,000. If we multiply 50,000 times the twelve baskets, 50,000 x 12 = 600,000.

Again, there were two fish, five loaves of bread, five thousand men alone, and twelve baskets left over. The total was 600,000 when these numbers are multiplied, 2 x 5 x 5000 x 12 = 600,000.

What is eerie is that this is *the exact number* recorded in the book of Exodus, which is the second book of Moses. When Moses led the people out of Egypt, there were 600,000 men alone, not including women and children. From the passages of Exodus to Matthew, the women and children were not included in the number.

> That night the people of Israel left Rameses and started for Succoth. There were about 600,000 men, plus all the women and children. (Ex. 12:37 NLT)

If you think this is just a coincidence, let's go back to the gospel of John. It records the reaction of the multitude after this miraculous feeding.

> Then those men, when they had seen the miracle that Jesus did, said, This is of a truth that prophet that should come into the world. When Jesus therefore perceived that they would come and take him by force, to make him a king, he departed again into a mountain himself alone. (John 6:14–15 KJV)

When Jesus perceived this hunger and desperate desire for Him to be the promised Messiah in triumph and power, He left the scene immediately. In the text, "that prophet" is a Mosaic reference to the coming Messiah. This power demonstrated was the Joseph Principle of multiplication. How do I know this? The sum, added up, is four factors (the 2, 5, 5,000, and 12), and the lesson of power was shown for His disciples, more so than for the people. Jesus, *the greater 1,* and the disciples, *the lesser 1 (11),* served the people in desperate need, after the disciples were on the mountain with Jesus for three days. That is 4 x 11. But we also see the sum of 44 with Jesus' disciples, as a group, serving as the greater ones, and the people as one group (the lesser 1s; therefore, 11, as well), times the four factors (the bread, the fish, the men, and the baskets), thus 11 x 4 = 44!

Jesus demonstrated before His disciples and followers how grace can be multiplied by the hand of the Almighty. This unique insight is *the Joseph Principle,* or the 44 factor, at its best. This leads us further to uncover a new dimension of grace in the prophet from Galilee in this next chapter (Mark 1:9).

CHAPTER 9

ANOTHER DIMENSION OF MULTIPLIED GRACE

Grace and peace be multiplied to you in the knowledge of
God and of Jesus our Lord. (2 Peter 1:2 NKJV)

In earlier chapters, we learned that the name *Joseph* means *to
add on*, which alludes to the fact that once Rachel finally had a
successful birth after many years of barrenness and longing, she then
believed she would bear more children, especially boys, in the future.
Finally, God had answered her prayers and desperate desires.

We have clearly shared how Joseph was a prophet-like protégé
worth waiting for. Even though Rachel died at the birth of her second
born, her prayers were and still are being answered, just as the name
she gave her first son was *future-bearing*, or prophetic. Joseph lived a life
that personified a messiah. He was a savior-deliverer of his own people,
the Egyptians, and of the neighboring nations, who successfully traded
food supplies during the seven-year drought. He was, through the
promotion and words of Pharaoh, placed into the most powerful role
and authority in the known world of that time. I believe that Rachel's
name for Joseph was the prophecy of destiny-in-waiting. I believe his
name has several dimensions, including that of the Messiah to come.
Or had the Messiah already come, and was overlooked as such?

King Solomon of Israel has long been considered as the wisest man who ever lived. He wrote the book of Ecclesiastes about his thoughts and considerations of life, after declining spiritually. In the opening chapters, he refers to the prophecy law of *repeated history*. I first learned these principles from the teaching of Dr. Perry Stone of Cleveland, Tennessee, who led the media ministry of *The Voice of Evangelism* in the late 1990s and has since, expanded tremendously until this day.

> The thing that has been—it is what will be again, and that which has been done is that which will be done again; and there is nothing new under the sun. Is there a thing of which it may be said, See, this is new? It has already been, in the vast ages of time [recorded or unrecorded] which were before us. (Eccl. 1:9–10, AMP)

> History merely repeats itself. It has all been done before. Nothing under the sun is truly new. Sometimes people say, "Here is something new!" But actually it is old; nothing is ever truly new. (Eccl. 1:9–10 NLT)

The New Living Translation tells us that history merely repeats itself. Solomon was referencing life in general, not actualities, like the same person doing the exact thing in a previous life. He was referring to the spirit of the situation—the principal aspects of people, places, or things. Ecclesiastes 3:15 also affirms this same truth: "Whatever is has already been, and what will be has been before; and God will call the past to account" (NIV).

I would like to share some comparisons of Jesus of Nazareth to Joseph of Egypt. There is absolutely no way the gospel writers made up this phenomenon, these character traits, and these events so that the likes of me could discover such things. The New Testament writers beyond the four gospels—including Paul, James, Luke, John, and Peter—did not even refer to the comparison. But I believe it was always in the mind of the Creator, who waited until it was time for us to recognize it. There is no formal statement in the holy writings or proof that this was known before now; therefore, inserted to create worldwide deception.

For instance, Jesus' life and eternal priesthood is compared to that of Moses in the book of Hebrews. Jesus made reference to King Solomon, King David, and other prophets in comparison to Himself. But the scribes, prophets, or New Testament writers (recording letters and writings after the life of Jesus of Nazareth) never ascertained a biblical comparison of the two.

I am not an original by any means concerning this comparison in the last several decades, if not centuries. When the Lord spoke to me in October 2005, I began to create and record this comparison chart, only to find others in like fashion. That was not deflation to me; that was *affirmative proof*! By discovering that others had written and observed the same, I received more confirmation that what the Almighty spoke to my heart was true.

Let's consider their lives as recorded and how they seem to intertwine. In my research, I found a list of ninety-nine comparisons. Though I did not take information from the sheet, I know I had come across over fifty during my own research of the Scriptures. Here is a reduced number of my findings, for your reference:

44 Similarities between the Life of Joseph Compared to the Life of Jesus Christ

1. Both were favorite and firstborn sons—Joseph to Rachel and Jesus to Mary (Matt. 1:25).
2. Both were rejected by their brethren (John 1:11; 7:3–5).
3. Both suffered immensely; Joseph through slavery and separation from his household and father, and Jesus through the Garden of Gethsemane, false trial, and crucifixion (John 19:16–30).
4. Both lived in Egypt for a period in their lives (Matt. 2:13–21).

5. Both experienced death-defying moments before their life expectancy; Joseph with his brother's plot and Potiphar's wife and Jesus' many near-death episodes (Luke 4:28–31; John 11:39–43).

6. Both were highly exalted as second in command by their superiors; Joseph by Pharaoh and Jesus by the Father of glory at His baptism (Matt. 3:16–17).

7. Both were thirty years old at the time of their great exaltation. The age of thirty was the Mosaic allowance for a priest to come into the fullness of his office and practice in the temple (Luke 3:23).

8. Both were given new names. Joseph's name was changed to Zaphnath-paaneah, by Pharaoh; and Jesus will have a new name no man knows but Him and the Father (Rev. 19:12–17).

9. Both were given spiritual wives after their exaltation. Joseph was given the priest's daughter, while John the Baptist referred to Jesus as the bridegroom, and Paul referred to the church as his spiritual bride (Luke 3:28–29; Eph. 5:21–33).

10. Joseph married an appointed Egyptian woman; therefore she was a Gentile—a non-Jewish person. Jesus is married to the church by covenant, primarily made up of Gentile believers (Eph. 2:16–20; 5:22–32).

11. Just as Joseph loved and favored his nearer-to-kin younger brother, Benjamin, over his other eleven brothers who, together, made up the twelve tribes of Israel. Jesus also loved and catered the most to His youngest disciple, John, of the core twelve disciples (Gen. 45:22; John 21:7, 20).

12. Both bore children by inheritance. Joseph had two sons, and Jesus inherits Jews and Gentiles (John 1:12; Eph. 2:11–20).

13. Neither were recognized by their brethren for a period of time (John 1:11–12).

14. They were both separated from their brethren, only to be reunited with them in joy (John 16:16–22, 20:19–20).

15. Both of their Fathers received blood as the evidence of their death (Jacob in being deceived; Jehovah according to Isaiah 53:9–12).

16. Both Fathers agonized at the death of their sons. It is recorded that the final 3 of the six hours that Jesus suffered in his crucifixion, there was prevailing darkness in the afternoon. Even though Joseph was yet alive, he was dead in his father's eyes. The word *death* also means *separation* (Matt. 27:45–46).

17. Both were sold for silver and traded for the price of a slave in their day. (Matt. 26:14–15).

18. Both had mothers who adored them. Joseph was not just Jacob's favorite; he was Rachel's firstborn, like Jesus was the firstborn of the Virgin Mary (Luke 2:4–7).

19. Their brothers in their own households did not care for them (John 7:1–5).

20. Both were sent to preserve great multitude in the world (John 3:16).

21. Both were wrongly accused, and lies were told about them (Mark 14:53–57).

22. Neither received a fair trial (John 18:28–32).

23. Both were extremely gifted with wisdom to interpret dreams and mysteries (Matt. 13:10–15; 22:15–22).

24. Both prospered in everything they did (Luke 2:41–52).

25. Each had a Jewish brother who tried to preserve their life; Joseph had Reuben, and Jesus had Nicodemus (John 7:45–52).

26. Because of dreams, both ended up living in Egypt (Matt. 2:13–15).

27. Both suffered alongside other accused men; one received life imprisonment, and the other received death as the verdict (Luke 23:39–43).

28. Both did or will administrate from a high office of influence during seven years of tribulation that will try the world (Matt. 25:31–46).

29. Both had their coats or robes stripped from them (Matt. 27:26–28).
30. Both Joseph and Jesus spent time in jail (Matt. 27:15–17).
31. Joseph interpreted dreams of men in jail, which determined their earthly destiny; Jesus preached to the spirits in prison, in the heart of the earth, and He determined their earthly and eternal destiny. (I Peter 3:18-20)
32. Both were given a name above every name in the land (Phil. 2:9–11)
33. Both were highly exalted in the midst of their brethren, who supposed them as dead, never to see them again.
34. Joseph conquered the pit and the jail upon promotion, just as Jesus conquered death, hell and the grave (Rev. 1:18)
35. Both were reunited with their Fathers after the sentence of death was given or carried out (John 14:28; Acts 1:9–11)
36. Both fathers were highly pleased with their sons (Matt. 3:16–17)
37. Joseph became a savior and lord of his master's goods with all authority; Jesus lived out his name and became the Savior and Lord with all authority unto the Father of glory (Matt. 28:18)
38. Joseph became a messiah-type; Jesus will become a Joseph-type and will reign as the Messiah (Acts 1:9–11; Rev. 19:11–16).
39. Everyone was commanded to bow before Joseph under the pharaoh's orders, and everyone will bow before Jesus one day by the command of the Father (Phil. 2:9–11).
40. Jacob was the father of Joseph of Egypt. The father of Joseph, Jesus' stepfather, was Jacob (Matt. 1:15–16).
41. Both were filled with the self-evident Spirit of God. Pharaoh acknowledged it in Joseph, while the life of Jesus was self-evident (John 3:33–35).
42. Joseph was envied by his brothers, the patriarchs, the first time, then was fully embraced the second time (second trip to Egypt), once he was revealed in all the glory of Egypt. So

it is with the Christ: He will be fully embraced by the nation Israel in all the glory of his Second Coming (Zech. 13:6–7).

43. Jacob prophesied over Joseph's future exaltation. God prophesied over Jesus' exaltation through the Old Testament prophets (Luke 22:44).

44. Both Joseph and Jesus received wounds in their feet and hands—Joseph during his journey in chains to Egypt, and Jesus through His crucifixion (Ps. 105:17–18; John 19:17–18).

These are but a few of the commonalities between the life of Joseph and the life of Jesus. Also concerning Jesus' genealogy, in the line of his mother Mary (Luke 3:23-38), isn't it ironic that the name Joseph appears exactly four times—no more, no less? SMH! Besides the number four being revealed, the number *three* is very precious in the life of Jesus and Christian believers concerning the belief in His resurrection after three days. But maybe even a more-prophetic sequence is that the life of Jesus was set in three stages—that of prophet, priest, and king. The life of Joseph was set in three stages also—that of a favored youth among the sons of Jacob, a life of slavery in the midst of favor with divine attributes (administrator and interpreter of dreams), and then as the most powerful leader of the known world, next to the throne of the pharaoh of Egypt. Obviously, the third stage of the life of Jesus is yet to be fulfilled, but His triumphant entry into Jerusalem through the east gate from the Mount of Olives was surely a practice run for his future that lies just ahead (Zech. 9:9; Matt. 21:1–11).

As we consider this next phase of hidden and mysterious wisdom, I would like you to read the famous words of Matthew 10:28–30, found in the New Testament.

> Come to me, all of you who are struggling and burdened, and I will give you rest. Take my yoke upon you and learn from me, because I am gentle and humble in heart, and you will find rest for your souls. For my yoke is easy, and my burden is light. (CJB)

Over fifteen years ago, Dr. Chuck Missler shared a powerful insight that gave further credence to the unique order set in the Scriptures showing evidence of a divine hand behind the conclusions.[51] He discovered a unique prophetic pattern found in the recorded generations, from Adam to Noah. The names are listed in the book of Genesis 5. Knowing the significance of names, especially in the Hebrew tradition, he observed the following with their original meanings:

1. Adam: "man"
2. Seth: "appointed"
3. Enos: "mortal or frail"
4. Kenanan: "sorrow"
5. Mahalael: "blessed or to be praised"
6. Jared: "shall come down"
7. Enoch: "teaching"
8. Methuselah: "his death shall bring forth"
9. Lamech: "despairing"
10. Noah: "rest"

Knowing New Testament doctrine, he was able to see an undeniable sequence with a hidden truth, when listing the names together with the added interjections. It reads, "Mankind appointed to mortal sorrow, but the Blessed shall come down, teaching that his death shall bring forth the despairing rest."[52]

Please understand that Moses, the prophets, and multitudes of scholars never observed this sequence. The listed names do not represent all firstborn children but simply projects the lineage of Noah, of his family tree. However, all those connected to Adam, all the way down to Noah, make up a unique hidden message of prophecy.

[51] Missler, Chuck. "A Hidden Message: The Gospel in Genesis." Koinonia House, n.d. Web. 15 Jan. 2014. http://www.khouse.org/articles/1996/44/.
[52] Ibid.

Let's consider this powerful layout. Almighty God had to oversee ten generations, and the Bible describes that they lived a very long time and had lots of children, yet the Scripture lists only the ones leading up to Noah. These words, chronologically put together, surpass the great man that even Noah became. Apparently the hidden prophetic message speaks of a god-like one who would visit the earth in the form of a man and sacrificially give His life to heal sin-sick humanity.

Were the words of Jesus in Matthew 11:28–30 set in a red-lettered edition of the Bible two thousand years ago? How does a two thousand–year-old message coincide with a seemingly unconnected storyline of Noah's ark, which happened over four thousand years ago? Was this simply understood in those days, or was it only discovered some two or so decades ago? I would like to say to Dr. Chuck Missler of Koinonia Institute that this is one of the most dynamic insights I have ever come across in all my years of study. To God be the glory for such illumination of knowledge and discovery!

Along with many, I have been greatly aided by the knowledge of Dr. Perry Stone, in reference to numerical insight on Jesus of Nazareth ruling in what could be considered "The Forty-Fourth Generation." First, we know that according to Matthew's genealogy of the birth of Jesus, he is the forty-second generation from Abraham, who was progenitor of many nations, but primarily the Hebrew people (Matt. 1:17). First Peter 2 then declares that the church, made up of Jews and Gentile followers, is a "chosen generation"; therefore, we are the forty-third generation (the church for two thousand years).

> But you *are* a chosen generation, a royal priesthood, a holy nation, His own special people, that you may proclaim the praises of Him who called you out of darkness into His marvelous light. (1 Peter 2:9 NKJV)

When Christ returns as the Messiah as promised in Isaiah 9:6–7, He will return to inherit all things as the forty-fourth generation. Now all I have shared can be debated, but some might question this logic of counting Jesus as the forty-second generation, who is returning to reclaim the forty-fourth generation fulfillment. However, something just as controversial occurred similar to this in the succession of presidents in US history. Grover Cleveland is the only president who served one four-year term in office as the twenty-second president, then lost the twenty-third election candidacy, only to come back and serve an additional four years as the twenty-fourth president. The debate of whether he should be only counted as *one* president is understood but useless. They were two separate terms—period.

Since we are speaking about Jesus as the possible Messiah and the US presidency, it is interesting that in the divisions of the book of Psalms, prophetically, Psalm 22 speaks of a suffering servant who died a tragic death for the people, and Psalm 24 prophesies the triumphant King-Messiah coming in great glory, who cannot be denied.

In between the two, Psalm 23 is one of the most-beloved passages throughout the monotheistic faiths of Christianity and Judaism, depicting an ever-present relationship between the Shepherd and his flock of followers. So between the suffering Messiah and the victorious Messiah, we are ever loving and experiencing Psalm 23 in all its dimensions, as His sheep (John 10:27).

Then the gospel of Matthew refers to the time the Messiah comes back as "the regeneration" (Matt. 19:28). I believe that the regeneration is the coming forty-fourth generation and is numerically represented by the Messiah's insignia: 44. Greater elaboration will occur in follow-up teaching in the few remaining chapters.

In gematria, the name *Jesus* in its Greek transliteration has a numerical sum of 888. The number 8 represents *a new beginning*. These triple 8s represent a brand-new era of spiritual, social, and political dynamics that the world has longed for.

Just as some question the truth of this presentation and its conclusions, many questioned Jesus of Nazareth in His day wondering just who He really was. I believe the Joseph Principle surfaced in this negative climate when people wondered, is He the Messiah, or isn't He? In Mark 6:1–4, we have the charted testimony of the people.

Then He went out from there and came to His own
country, and His disciples followed Him. And when the
Sabbath had come, He began to teach in the synagogue.
And many hearing *Him* were astonished, saying, "Where
did this Man *get* these things? And what wisdom *is*
this which is given to Him, that such mighty works
are performed by His hands! Is this not the carpenter,
the Son of Mary, and brother of James, and Joses, and
of Juda, and Simon? And are not His sisters here with
us?" So they were offended at Him. But Jesus said to
them, "A prophet is not without honor except in his own
country, among his own relatives, and in his own house."
(Mark 6:1–4 NKJV)

We quickly notice that they asked four questions, and we
know this number is significant concerning the Joseph Principle.
But in the midst of the third question, we notice a hidden treasure
concerning this principle. "Is this not the carpenter (Jesus' trade
from his stepfather Joseph), the Son of Mary (his miraculous birth),
and brother of James, and Joses, of Juda, and Simon?" (v. 3). They
named his male siblings in this verse, and then they asked the fourth
question about his sisters still living among them. But they *named
the four brothers!* The names fit the scenario well.

1. James
2. Joses
3. Judas
4. Simon

Let's look at the Hebrew-originated names:

1. James is a transliteration of *Jacob*, who was Joseph's father.
2. Joses is another name for *Joseph.*
3. Judas is another reference for the name *Judah.*

4. Simon is a reference to the name *Simeon,* coincidentally, Joseph's brother who was held for ransom in Egypt, while his brethren returned home the first time.

We have *four* questions about Jesus' siblings, who happen to be *four* males, without specific mention of his sisters. That's four brothers' names inside of the four questions asked. We know that the number 44 is a 4 inside of a 4, by digits, in the spirit of gematria. On top of this, every name coincides with the biblical story of Joseph of Egypt. The story starts with Jesus and His disciples coming back into His own hometown. The number 11, right? Jesus is *the greater 1,* and the group is *the lesser 1.* The number 11, times the 4 questions, equals 44. We also have the four brothers, including James, mentioned in the third question. This is interesting because the name *Jacob* or *James* is referenced, and Jacob is the third generation of Abraham (after Isaac), who brought the family down to Egypt in the midst of the drought. So while they were questioning, *"Who is this Jesus?"* is of their hometown of Nazareth, the answer was bleeding out, although in a mysterious fashion.

Let us add a few details of Rachel, the beloved, yet deprived, wife of Jacob. As she was about to give birth to her second son, things went terribly wrong. Here we may wonder, why does God allow bad things to happen to good people? I mean, let's be honest … you cannot be living more in the will of God than Rachel was. Look who she was married to, who she was raising, and she only wanted to participate in one of life's most precious gifts— bringing a child into the world. Wasn't God watching over her? He surely watched over the baby she delivered and named him Benoni (Gen. 35:16–20).

The beloved Rachel lost her life instead, and it practically ripped out the heart of Jacob. Joseph (who is believed to be around seven years old at the time) and the entire household was also heartbroken. Though we may not understand the reasons behind this, we know God is good and He will make up the differences, if we let Him.

Many times we must endure suffering before achieving our greatest triumphs. Rachel lost her life on earth, but I believe her spirit is well cared for in paradise.

When Rachel died, the caravan of this wealthy nomadic family was on their way to Ephrath, the former name of what became the city of Bethlehem. Rachel was buried and memorialized with a shrine in the place where she died. As she died, she named her baby boy *Ben-o-ni,* meaning "the son of my sorrow."[53] Jacob stepped in and said, "No, we will name him Benjamin" (Gen. 35:18). The name *Benjamin* means *the son of my right hand.* Jacob foresaw, in great hope, that the tragedy would be turned into a triumph. This is nothing more than the faith he had developed in his God.

Jesus was born in Bethlehem, after caravanning with his parents Mary and Joseph, on behalf of a decree made by Caesar Augustus. They had barely made it to the inn, which had no available spaces. After thirty-three years, He was hung on an old rugged cross made of beams and was crucified, while his mother, the disciple John, and other faithful women witnessed this horror. Jesus became "the son of my sorrow" (Gen. 35:18). But according to faith and other proofs, He arose, with all power in His hands, as predicted by the prophets. He is now on the right hand of the Father, waiting for the time of His triumphant return.

So we end this chapter with a question worthy of deep consideration: Was the former name of *Benoni,* and the eventual name of *Benjamin,* a foretold prophecy of the same person, fulfilling two paradoxes of life? I believe so. And the same spirit of the Joseph Principle was guiding this process of redemption.

Most rabbis will not recognize Jesus of Nazareth as the promised Messiah because He did not place the government on His shoulders, providing deliverance for the physical nation of Israel. Yet it is the oral interpretation of a few that there is the suffering episode of the Messiah, referred to as "Messiah Ben Joseph," and the triumphant

[53] http://www.sheknows.com/baby-names/name/benoni.

Messiah, called "Messiah Ben David."[54] Messiah Ben Joseph possibly is the one characterized and recognized as Jacob's son Joseph, the one who suffers for the people before creating an oasis for his people. Messiah Ben David sees entitlement in the coming Messiah, the son of David, as referenced in Ezekiel 37, and He will bind the nation back to its fullness of ancient promises, with Israel being the light of the world.

I also recognize the two positions, but along with many Gentiles and a growing camp of Jews, by faith, we see the same person, as Jacob renamed him Benjamin.

That's exactly what is in the New Testament in the book of Matthew, while Jesus was on trial with the Sanhedrin, and the high priest was leading the charge of blasphemy against Jesus of Nazareth.

> But Jesus was silent and made no reply. Then the high priest asked him, "Are you the Messiah, the Son of the Blessed One?" Jesus said, "I AM. And you will see the Son of Man seated in the place of power at God's right hand and coming on the clouds of heaven." Then the high priest tore his clothing to show his horror and said, "Why do we need other witnesses? (Mark 14:61–63 NLT)

Simply put, it is the true Christian's belief that in the first manifestation of Messiah Ben Joseph, He suffered for the sins of the world, both Jew and Gentile alike. Even His birth name came from the angelic messenger, "And thou shall call is name Jesus" (Matt. 1:21 KJV). Jesus means *Savior*, "[One who] shall save his people from their sins." (Matt. 1:21 KJV).

The high priest prophesied or spoke a word supposedly from the Spirit of God that one should die for the good of the nation.

---

[54] "The Exalted Messiah Ben David." n.d. *Menorah Ministries*. Retrieved February 05, 2014, from http://www.menorah.org/tembd14.html.

If we let him thus alone, all men will believe on him: and the Romans shall come and take away both our place and nation. And one of them, named Caiaphas, being the high priest that same year, said unto them, ye know nothing at all, Nor consider that it is expedient for us, that one man should die for the people, and that the whole nation perish not. And this spake he not of himself: but being high priest that year, he prophesied that Jesus should die for that nation; And not for that nation only, but that also he should gather together in one the children of God that were scattered abroad. (John 11:48–52 KJV)

Whether it was truly the Spirit of God or not, it is tantalizing to understand how the Lord God reveals truth through the hearts of men, even when evil or ill intentions are the case. It is like the story of Joseph: what his brothers meant for evil, God ultimately turned it around to bring forth salvation to whosoever would believe and receive Him as Messiah Ben Joseph. But let it be known that Messiah Ben David is now getting ready to showcase in a few more years to come, that Superman actually looks like Clark Kent in everyday clothes, working as a newspaper reporter, according to the likes of myself. As they say, don't get mad at the mailman; he is just delivering the mail!

CHAPTER 10

JOSEPH AND THE WINGS OF AMERICA

It is no secret that the United States of America has been a second homeland for many cultures and races by immigration, and New York City is the capital of this strategic incoming population. And why not? That is where the Statue of Liberty resides, symbolizing the home of the brave and the land of the free. Besides all the great and extremely tragic struggles to make and maintain our country's freedom, it was founded by many Europeans (namely the Puritans of New England and the Pennsylvania Friends, also known as Quakers). They embodied, developed, and established the belief that religious, as well as political, liberties should be the mainstay of the new land.

This Protestant revolution called this glorious hope of a new beginning as *the New Jerusalem* and *the Promised Land*. They named cities, towns, and counties in the early seventeenth and eighteenth centuries after Hebrew names, which grew from the influence of the holy canon in the life of these early settlers. Providence (Rhode Island) and Philadelphia (Pennsylvania) are names taken from the book of Revelation, and many towns in the region are called Galilee and Bethlehem. Jamestown, Virginia, the earliest permanent settlement, was named in honor of King James I, who sat on the throne of England and who authorized the most popular English transliteration of our time, *the King James Version of the Holy Bible*. A nice touch of history concerning the roots of Virginia and the nation is found in the *Root 52 Virginia Prayer Guide*. This in-depth briefing provides some interesting details, as it relates to the early settlements of the United States of America, via the state grounds of Virginia.

> Cape Henry is a point of land at the mouth and entrance to the Chesapeake Bay. This site was the first landing in the new world for the settlers and crew of the group of the Virginia Company that would become the first English permanent settlement at Jamestown in 1607. The Virginia Company under the 1601 Charter was the fourth try in England's effort to establish a colony in the new world. The settlers (105) and seamen (40) set sail from England December 20, 1606. After four storm-tossed months at sea, the three ships, Susan Constant, Godspeed, and the Discovery arrived. They were under the leadership of Captain Christopher Newport.
>
> The ships arrived April 26, 1607 with the first landing party coming ashore. Then Rev. Robert Hunt, because of strife aboard the ship, called for three days of prayer and fasting. The company came ashore April 29, 1607, planted a wooden cross, and had a time of thanksgiving, prayer, and worship. Rev. Robert Hunt spoke these words: "From these very shores the Gospel shall go forth to not only this New World but the entire world." The Lord has spoken to many intercessors that "His cross was and is the gateway into this country." [55]

---

[55] Grady, Sandy. USRPN-VA, comp. "Virginia Root 52 Prayer Guide." *General International Prayer School* (2010): n. p. Web. 07 Jan. 2014. Founders, Mike and Cindy Jacobs.

Speaking of the gateway into this country, we can quickly see the providential means of the Joseph Principle. Again, without gross exaggeration or fables, we seek to know the blueprint of evidence concerning the hand of the Lord.

1. The ships set sail as the fourth try in England's effort to establish the first English permanent settlement at Jamestown
2. The voyage of the three ships took about four months
3. Forty seamen empowered the sail and guidance of the ships
4. The words of Reverend Robert Hunt,[56] the first vicar of the settlement community, pronounces that the gospel shall go forth, not only in the new land, but into the whole world, from off these very shores. The Christian gospel is the good news that Jesus is the Messiah.

He was convinced that it needed and was going to happen on those shorelines, around the world.

The fourth try, the forty seamen, and the four months it took to travel from the Old World to the New World all affirm the Joseph Principle. In accordance with the spirit of gematria, we easily see the number 4, if not 44. Maybe more compelling is Rev. Robert's request, in seeing strive and chaos of the trip taking its toll on the passengers, convincingly delayed the shoreline settlement a few days. Therefore, they touched the ground 3 days later, and the date was April 29th. April is the fourth month; the 29th day is eleven, as two plus nine (2+9) in the second step of reduced integral value. What do we have? 4 times 11 equal 44!

The Joseph Principle is powerful because, as I have indicated, it has eternal implications, particularly regarding Joseph's second dream, in which the sun and the moon bowed down to him. These timekeepers will continuously serve as a backdrop for perpetual blessings. I should note for you that the word *principle* also points to

---

[56] Ibid.

what takes place from the beginning of a thing. Joseph's first dream carries some "first things first" characteristics that should not be overlooked. The sheaves that stood were from either a wheat or barley harvest; therefore, they were the result of planting a field. Seed had to be sown to bring about the eventual harvest.

As we pointed out in the book of Job, this reveals how the Lord God considers and searches out before He decides how to go about a law or principle on the earth. The knowledge is not isolated but rather fits into the arrangement of the heavens, as well as into the ecology of the earth. In other words, the Joseph Principle is connected to the principle of planting first, to harvest later. In order to begin the government of Israel, God started by calling Abraham out from the culture he was a part of to begin a new nation (Gen. 12:1–3). Then He revealed to Abraham that He was going to allow the nation, like a vineyard, to be replanted and fertilized in a greater nation before bringing them out after about four hundred years. In so doing, God allowed and oversaw the suffering, but ultimately the planting, of Joseph in the land of Egypt.

Even when the nation of Israel split and the monotheistic (belief in the one true living God) nation slipped into pagan worship, they eventually suffered by losing wars and being ravaged by their enemies underneath severe correction, the promises of God that were first given to Abraham remained steadfast. Even when God prophesied over the sons through the mouth of their father Jacob, which spoke to their future expectations, He foresaw a time of disobedience and fulfilled His warning that He would scatter the nation throughout the earth.[57] Assyria captured and plundered the north (Joseph/Ephraim) in the year 722 BC, and Judah (the south) went down to Babylon in 586 BC, as both chose to reject the Lord their God, choosing instead false idols and treacherous actions.

---

[57] "History of Ancient Israel." *Israel's and Judah's Captivity and Judah's Return.* Stephen Ricker, n.d. Web. 15 Jan. 2014. http://www.stephenricker.com/study/israel_history.html.

It shall be also carried unto Assyria for a present to King Jareb: Ephraim shall receive shame, and Israel shall be ashamed of his own counsel. (Hos. 10:16 KJV)

But in the scattering, a seed still forms and creates within itself the ability to reproduce new life. So before obedience, God already speaks a blessing, and the blessing will remain intact. If the individual (or singular nation) participates in the rebellion and wrongdoing, it will lose out and does not benefit from what was already spoken (the Joseph blessing). Manassas and Ephraim were supplanted in the twelve tribes of Israel, as Jacob adopted them and counted them as his own. Simply put, Joseph's sons with the birthright represented the double blessing of Joseph's life. As the nations grew and eventually split, the northern tribes were prophetically called *Israel* or *Ephraim*. When the northern tribes were taken in Assyrian captivity in 722 BC, they were intermixed with the people of that area and culture. It is in this assimilation that the lost tribes of Israel scattered beyond the north and the Baltic as a race and people. There are many historians who believe that the development of England was seeded by these nomadic people of the lost tribes of the north.

Yet I will leave a remnant, so that you may have *some* who escape the sword among the nations, when you are scattered through the countries. (Ezek. 6:8 KJV)

The Jews faced ultimate judgment and have been scattered throughout the world.

We now notice the Joseph Principle begins to emerge again, as the groups migrate northwest over the centuries. The holy writ states something very interesting, of which I believe people have very little knowledge. I will paraphrase the passage of Scripture that is spoken by the Lord through the prophet Amos, "The Lord does nothing in the Earth, without choosing first to speak with an oracle (male or female prophet) first about it" (Amos 3:7). "Before it is done, the LORD foreknows it, and determines its end" (Isa. 46:10). The recording prophet, like Daniel, then chronicles through the scribes and priesthood to preserve the writings. Thus, it was prerecorded that these nations would become world powers in the Middle Eastern or Mediterranean region, even before they did so. All overtook Israel in one way or another. We are cutting through and summarizing world history as it relates to all, but ultimately, the promises of God to Israel begin with Abraham to Joseph and King David.

Let's continue. Just as the ships, the Susan Constant, Godspeed, and the Discovery had to travel across the deep blue waters of the Atlantic Ocean, we are now going to have to travel together through some heavy knowledge and considerations, concerning the Joseph Principle, so hold on with your thinking caps!

Daniel recorded these prophesized nations to gain control (according to Daniel, chapters 2 and 7) by the use of symbolic language and dream interpretation for King Nebuchadnezzar of Babylon. Chapter 2 speaks of King Nebuchadnezzar's dream and Daniel's interpretation of the dream, and chapter 7 records Daniel's affirmation of the dream as symbolism, which confirms the King of Babylon's dream. We can see that the dreams actually occurred in chronological order:

> Daniel spoke, saying, "I saw in my vision by night, and behold, the four winds of heaven were stirring up the Great Sea. And four great beasts came up from the sea, each different from the other. The first *was* like a lion, and had eagle's wings. I watched till its wings were plucked off; and it was lifted up from the Earth and made to stand on two feet like a man, and a man's heart was given to it. And suddenly another beast, a second, like a bear. It was raised up on one side, and *had* three ribs in its mouth between its teeth. And they said thus to it: 'Arise, devour much flesh!' After this I looked, and there was another, like a leopard, which had on its back four wings of a bird. The beast also had four heads, and dominion was given to it. After this

I saw in the night visions, and behold, a fourth beast, dreadful and terrible, exceedingly strong. It had huge iron teeth; it was devouring, breaking in pieces, and trampling the residue with its feet. It *was* different from all the beasts that *were* before it, and it had ten horns. (Dan. 7:2–7 KJV)

In these Scriptures, we again find a reference to four important world powers:

1. Babylon (the lion)
2. The Medes and Persians (the bear)
3. Greece (the leopard)
4. The Romans (the fourth beast)

The statue in Nebuchadnezzar's dream has multiple levels of earthly materials that speak of the strength of the nation and its world conquest. The use of animals in Daniel's dream symbolizes the character of the nations that will have dominion for a period of time. It is simply amazing that these precise prophecies not only came true, but let's observe how Daniel and Joseph's relationships with foreign sovereignties emerge. Here is a list of some similarities:

1. Joseph and Daniel were Jews taken captive.
2. Both men had the unique gift of having and interpreting prophetic dreams.
3. Both men arose to notoriety among dominant cultures in which their people were considered inferior by captivity.
4. Both were summoned to the palace courts to be heard and to interpret dreams.
5. Both were immediately exalted for the God of heavens being with them and for having the wisdom to help rule the land.
6. Both Gentile kings had dreams that bothered them so badly that they went to extremes before the Hebrew men were summoned.
7. Both dream interpretations predicted the future of the nation.

Dr. Perry Stone Jr.'s book *Plucking the Eagle's Wings* provides some of the most interesting facts about the strongly interwoven ties of the nation of Israel with the United States of America and its paralleled history.[58] His insights connected to the spiritual truths found in the book of Ecclesiastes, as stated earlier in the book. Just as history tends to repeat itself, so it is in Bible prophecy when a passage of Scripture has multiple settings. In other words, the situation described often has a future event involving like circumstances.

Inside the four kingdoms predicted above, there lies another modern-day application to the times leading up to today. In other words, even though the Roman Empire as we knew it came to an end around AD 400, there is another prophecy *within the prophecy* that unfolds like this. It is called *the law of double reference,* which reads as follows:

1. The lion of the Babylonians correlates with Great Britain, whose wings were detached due to the formation of the United States. The symbol of Great Britain is the lion.
2. The bear of the Medes and Persian Empire could represent Russia, which also uses and recognizes the bear as its symbol.
3. The leopard of Greece can be depicted as Germany because of Hitler's regime that shifted the modern world via Hitler and World War II, until he was stopped in 1945.
4. The final beast of the Romans can also depict a somewhat undetermined regime of an international government, which will affect the end of days as we know.

As stated in Daniel's dream, the modern consideration of Great Britain as a lion that has the wings of an eagle sounds intriguing. The prophecy mentions how the wings are plucked off, and planted in the soil, to rise as a man with a heart of compassion (Dan. 7:4). We can observe that the United States came out of Great Britain or England and was planted in the Americas. The United States is known as the

---

[58] Stone, 2001.

most benevolent, helping nation for those who are suffering or dealing with a natural disaster through our nonprofit organizations like the Red Cross and Christian paragroups who are committed to such. If you can agree with this possibility of preordained establishment and destiny, then what we just observed was a *lesser* 4 inside the predominant or *greater* number 4! In clarity, a 44!

This law of double reference is a seed of truth (prophecy) of repeated history, according to Ecclesiastes 1:9, "there is nothing new under the sun." Daniel's prophecy had a double meaning. It was a seed of truth, inside another seed of truth. Looking closer, it was four modern day governments inside four ancient governments; therefore, the Joseph Principle, revealing the 44 factor.

Many well-meaning believers over the centuries have expounded that the regions of Great Britain and England were populated with descendants of the northern tribes of Israel in their disbursement. I have read and researched this, and I still never gained peace that actually confirms this consideration. Regardless, we see the spiritual threads of Israel interwoven into the fabric of America, and we know the United States of America was first the seed of the thirteen colonies of England. From the foundation of the American Revolution, we see signs of all kinds that speak to a connection with the Joseph Principle or blessings upon the nation. Many of the early foundations of the nation were cultivated by those who were Jewish, even if it happened undercover.

There are signs that Christopher Columbus, founder of America in 1492 (the title given by historians), was actually a Jewish Italian who remained undercover because of threats of persecution. He grew up in Spain. He avoided initial ship voyages on the ninth day of Av, which in the history of the Jews, has proven to be a very bad omen on their historic calendar.

Haym Solomon, who served as a financial broker, raised the majority of the funding for the American Revolutionary War. Eventually God used this man to save the new nation from financial collapse. He was also under the conviction that in chapter 7 in the book of Daniel, which elaborates on Daniel's dream, the reference to eagles' wings being plucked from the lion was America breaking from England.[59] This conviction of thought was popular enough that it eventually led to the eagle being the sign of the American seal. The likes of Benjamin Franklin and Thomas Jefferson also used biblical references to underscore the theme and symbolism of a brand new nation. Both suggested different versions of a picture of Moses and the children of Israel escaping from the Egypt and Pharaoh's army, but the committee chose the eagle. The symbolic seal depicts the eagle having thirteen olive branches in one claw, standing for the desire of the thirteen established colonies (before official status as states) to remain at peace. But in the opposite talons, the eagle held arrows, depicting the nation and its militia would defend its new identity if war became necessary. This symbol appears on the back of every US dollar bill.

As many know, the Hebrew people are the descendants of Abraham, biologically born of Sarah, the mother of promise by a miracle angelic visitation as she became pregnant with Isaac. It was during this time that God visited Abraham with instructions to begin a sign of relationship through circumcision. This surgical procedure on the male child was to be performed from now on, as a sign of a covenant agreement between the Almighty and the people. The word *covenant* means *the cutting of the skin or flesh*. The word *British* actually means *the man of covenant*.

The number 13 reflects the thirteen colonies, while the nation of Israel was composed of thirteen tribes, including the priesthood of the tribe of Levi.

Robert Phillips contends that England represents Ephraim and Manasseh, the thirteenth tribe of Israel, in spirit.[60] He lists the following, including what I have already indicated:

- Thirteen states signed the Declaration of Independence.
- Thirteen stars are above the eagle on the American seal.

[59] Stone, 2001.
[60] Phillips, Robert. "Ephraim and Mannaseh: Role Reversal Refuted!" Editorial. http://www.ensignmessage.com/archives/ephraim.html. *The Ensign Message*, June 2005. Web. 12 Oct. 2013.

- Thirteen letters form the motto *E Pluribus Unum,* meaning *one of many.*
- Thirteen leaves are on the olive branch on the left talon.
- Thirteen olives also are on the left talon of the US seal.
- Thirteen arrows are on the right talon of the shield.
- Thirteen stripes are featured on the shield.
- Thirteen stars were on the original US flag, *Old Glory.*
- Thirteen stripes are still featured on the current flag of the United States.

This may not seem important, but it does seek the common thread of purpose and affiliation. Again, thirteen proved to be a good way to start, not a means to bad luck. It serves as a symbol of a divinely appointed beginning. In the Jewish culture, a boy is officially recognized as transitioning into an adult male at thirteen years of age, called a bar mitzvah. It was in like fashion that the infancy of America would be tested into manhood. Remember that the number 13 is the number 4 undercover, just like the numbers 22 and 31 in the spirit of gematria. By adding the single digits, we receive the sum of 4. Thus, we fulfill the meaning of the name *Joseph.*

In the fight for independence, the war lasted from 1777 till 1785, or approximately eight years and four months. The number 8 represents double 4s by addition. It is the number of new beginnings. When the famine finished its seven-year cycle of terror, Joseph was forty-four years old (double 4s by association), and it began a new life for him, as well as a sigh of relief for the people of his nation who had suffered through seven years of death and drought.

Many other nations came from or through England's reign. I am not belittling the historic connections of other nations to Great Britain or England, but I am merely focusing on how America carries a blessing through the likes of the Joseph Principle and its Hebrew origins.

The third uprising of the Third Reich of Germany, after the smoke cleared following Hitler's attempt at being a world power through the evil works of the holocaust, was a stepping stone of the rebirth of the nation of Israel as a one core nation of Jews. Now many Jews have returned to the homeland of their roots.

In speaking about the Abrahamic covenant, the United States, like the nation of Israel, faced a split between the North and the South, which led to the Civil War from 1861 till 1865. The man who had to face the ugliness of war and bloodshed was the elected sixteenth president of the United States. His name was befitting, *Abraham Lincoln*, whose first name after the Biblical progenitor means *father of many nations.*

Lincoln led under such duress—a government on the brink of bankruptcy, a man living with personal wounds in his life and marriage—yet he stood tall among men as our sixteenth president. The number 16 is 4 x 4, another way of showing a double 4 by multiples. After the North won the Civil War with Robert E. Lee's surrender to Ulysses S. Grant at the Appomattox Court House on April 9, 1865, Lincoln was accredited the reward for taking the bold steps of preserving the nation in a dire crisis. Though he was cut down by an assassin's bullet only a short time later, he left a legacy that will never be forgotten and will forever be appreciated.

As sad as it was for the nation to endure such a tragedy, it sounded the alert of repeated history. For another bottle was shattered when the likes of a young senator won the Democratic election to become the thirty-fifth president of the United States (3 + 5 = 8). In November 1963, that president was also gunned down, and brought the nation to its knees. What happens through the following comparisons of such is nothing short of eerie and seems to point toward the awareness and reality of destiny.[61]

- Both presidents were elected to the House of Representatives in '46, one hundred years apart.

[61] "Rosettasister's Weblog." *Rosettasisters Weblog.* N.p., n.d. Web. 15 Jan. 2014. http://rosettasister.wordpress.com/2008/12/14/dolley-madison-george-washington-the-tornado-and-the-burning-of-washington-in-1814/

- Both presidents were elected to the presidency in '60, one hundred years apart.
- Lincoln defeated incumbent Vice President John C. Breckenridge for the presidency; Kennedy defeated incumbent Vice President Richard M. Nixon for the presidency.
- Both men's predecessors left office in their seventies and retired to Pennsylvania. James Buchanan, whom Lincoln succeeded, retired to Lancaster Township; Dwight D. Eisenhower, whom Kennedy succeeded, retired to Gettysburg.
- Both of their vice presidents and successors were Southern Democrats named Johnson (Andrew Johnson and Lyndon Johnson) who were born in '08.
- Both presidents were concerned with the problems of black Americans and made their views strongly known in '63. Lincoln signed the Emancipation Proclamation in 1862, which became law in 1863. In 1963 Kennedy presented his reports to Congress on civil rights, and the same year, famous March on Washington for Jobs and Freedom occurred.
- Both Johnsons were succeeded as president in '69 by Republicans whose mothers were named Hannah.

These scenarios strongly affirm the *law of repeated history*, found in the book of Ecclesiastes (Eccl. 1:9). It should be noted that just as President Lincoln was named after the patriarch Abraham, this phenomenal comparison is approximately one hundred years apart, not unlike Abraham and Sarah miraculously had their baby boy when Abraham turned one hundred years old.

CHAPTER 11

THE PREDESTINATION OF THE FORTY-FOURTH PRESIDENT

The Weather Channel had a series called *When Weather Changed History*, and it acknowledges how sudden shifts in weather patterns in history have helped in determining the fate of how things worked out, for bad or for good.[62] According to this series, on August 25, 1815, the British were storming into Washington, DC, during the War of 1812 campaign. After 4,500 British troops overcame the approximately 7,000 unprofessional soldiers of the American army the day before, Washington was set ablaze, including the White House. President James Madison had to escape to safer ground. As the British proceeded to do the same damage the following day, a sudden tornado appeared and was so severe that it caused the British troops to retreat, saving the nation's capital at that time. Buildings still ablaze were spared as the heavy downpour put out the flames. Several of the British troops were killed by flying debris, and the British armies retreated to their ships, only to realize that several of the ships were damaged by the storm.

---

[62] When Weather Changed History. (n.d.). *The Weather Channel Programs.* Retrieved February 05, 2014, from http://www.weather.com/tv/programs/ When-Weather-Changed-History.html

As the United States approached election time in the 2008, a strong wind suddenly blew in the financial markets as fear gripped investors globally. On September 29 of that year, the market dropped a whopping 777 points on the Dow Jones Industrial Average in one session.[63] This type of panic came along with costly expenses and lives lost in a longer-than-anticipated Iraqi War. This discontentment created a greater wind of adversity for the Republican Party candidate who was running against the fresh breed of a polished speaker with a universal approach.

We have engaged in the scenario that the numerical value of 44 has so many unique facets that this book alone cannot cover its wide-range dimensions. But this numerical value is observed in one of the most historical events in modern times in America—the election of the nation's first black president.

For any man is to become the leader of the free world in a relatively short span of four years as a junior senator of the US Senate and an eight-year state senator of Illinois is simply outside the norm and an extraordinary feat. The election of Barack Hussein Obama as the forty-fourth US president was a surprise that only the heavens foreknew. After the presidency of William Jefferson Clinton, it appeared obvious that his wife, Hillary Rodham Clinton, popular former senator from the third-most-populated state of New York, was the Democratic choice to regain the White House. But such was not the case.

If this storyline had been mentioned just two years before the actual election, it would indeed have been a laughable scenario. The Clinton genre alone, with its political ties, should have been enough to subdue this new kid on the block of Washington politics. Chicago is one thing; Washington, DC quite another.

> For exaltation *comes* neither from the east, nor from the west, nor from the south. But God *is* the Judge: He puts down one, and exalts another. (Ps. 75:6–7 NKJV)

---

[63] *Stocks Take Record Tumble, Down 777 Points.* CBS News. N.d. *Stocks Take Record Tumble, Down 777 Points.* CBS Interactive, Inc., 29 Sept. 2008. Web. 13 Jan. 2014. http://www.cbsnews.com/news/stocks-take-record-tumble-down-777-points/.

It is God who exalts one above another. It was the Lord who chose King Saul, in spite of his life of compromise and eventually destructive decisions and oppressive jealousy toward David. So, whether the person is righteous or unrighteous, politically savvy or politically asinine, ultimately it is the Lord who chooses or allows a nation to be blessed or set up for judgment.

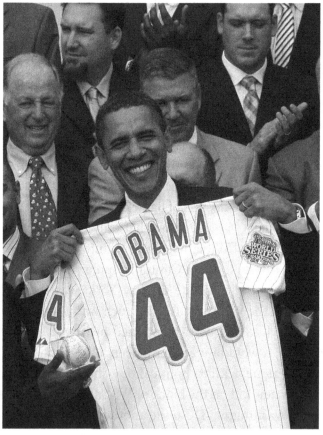

President Barack Obama held up a jersey at the White House and he was presented a ball with team signatures, presented by the Philadelphia Phillies, in reference to their 2008 World Series win. He also threw out the first pitch at the 80th Major League Baseball All Star Game, held in St. Louis, MO, on July 14, 2009. After the American League beat the National League, 4-3, that night, the overall series was now led by the National League, 40-38-2. Do you see a symbolic sequence of numbers that depict his presidency as well as the season we are now in? Photo accredited to Win Namee/ Getty Images.

There was a pharaoh who was right for the people when Joseph was exalted. Then there was another pharaoh on the throne who hardened his heart and made the land of Egypt a stockpile of rubbish, while the ten plagues ravaged the land, to release the nation of Israel from untold suffering. Beyond race, creed, culture, or pedigree, there is a purpose and a reason for such, sometimes beyond explanation at the time.

In step with the Joseph Principle, we have to always consider the numbers 4 and 11, which can readily be seen in the life of President Barack Obama. When we consider how Barack became the forty-fourth president in the year 2008, the facts stand out in front of us, now that we have on our new spiritual lens of the Joseph Principle.

Obama was born in the eighth month of the Julian calendar, in August. The number 8 is 2 sets of 4. He was born on the fourth day of August—again, a universal or world-related number. At the same time he was being officially nominated as the Democratic candidate, he turned forty-seven years old. With gematria considerations, 4 + 7 = 11. He turned forty-seven on August 4, 2008, which comes out to 11 (4 + 7), times 4 (his birth date), equals 44—the chronological number of the next president of the country. Before we say this is stretching it way too far in the occult of numerology, remember that 44 can also be hidden yet verified in the number 8 (4 + 4). This sequence of numerical relationships just happened to occur when the International Olympic Games was about to take place in China, where the number eight is magnified above all other numbers. Let's consider some of the happenstance.

Again, the year of the election pointed to a double 4, the year 2008. The number 8 is biblically defined as the number of new beginnings. A US presidential election always occurs at the same time of the Summer Olympics, which simultaneously occurs every four years. But the number 8 stands out by itself because of the turn of a millennium—a thousand year period. The Summer Olympics started in August, as normal, but nonetheless this is the eighth month. The games started on the eighth day. The opening ceremony was orchestrated at 8:00 p.m.! Now for this to even take place, it had to be in a country that honored the number 8 as its most significant number, namely Beijing, China.

In the Chinese culture, just like in biblical significance, the number 8 symbolizes prosperity and good fortune. It is not as if the Olympics are frequently held in China like the United States, which usually hosts the games about every thirty or so years. China – which was closed off from the Western involvement just four decades ago – served as a wonderful host for this international phenomenon competition. With China hosting its *first* Olympics ever, a record was broken that seemed impossible.

Mark Spitz won seven gold medals in swim events in Munich, Germany, in 1972. But the United States just happened to have a swimmer who could possibly duplicate the task, with the help of his teammates. Michael Phelps broke the record with eight gold medals in dramatic fashion. His swim teammate, Jason Lezak, had one of the greatest swims in his life to outswim arguably the second-best swimmer in the games, Alain Bernard of France, in the four by one hundred relay, to secure the possibility. The comeback victory by 0.08 was one of my most memorable moments in sports history. Even for the agnostic, this is something to think about. Why all the 8s, or two 4s? Consider the crossroad of facts: Why China during this particular time? How did all this just come together like tributaries flowing into the same ocean?

Consider, too, that Barack's name did not assist him at all in the political process. His name carried such a negative connotation at that time that it alone would normally have sunk his chances of being elected. *Barack Hussein Obama* is not the choicest name to have in the climate of America's present history against terrorism. The wars in Iraq and Afghanistan have created a very hostile environment for a name of Arabic origin. The wars have been exceedingly religious and unjust, with selfish political objectives. The truth is that it is a war against radical Islam, whose goal is world dominance in the name of the prophet Muhammad. After September 11, 2001, and the destruction of the famous Twin Towers of New York and the loss of about three thousand lives in three locations, the war on terror is now at the forefront of political considerations.

Barack consistently took hits in political consideration of his candidacy, as rumors circulated about his background, with a Muslim father and stepfather and his attendance in Islamic schools in Indonesia during his youth. His name, within context, actually accommodates his well-being. The number one nemesis at the time, besides Osama Bin Laden for a season, was Saddam Hussein.

The forty-fourth president's first name, *Barack*, means *blessed* or *blessed one*.[64] The origin is African, and its Hebrew form is *Baruch*. This additional translation alludes to *good-looking*. And yes, without a doubt, many consider Barack to be charming, likeable, and even good-looking. His ability to convey an idea and speak to the masses is compelling. But let's consider the rest.

His name, Hussein, is Arabic and is very popular in Muslim societies. *Hussein* is Arabic, and means *a gift of God, favorable*.[65] In the same context, Christians speak of the word *grace*. At the time of 9/11, the United States had distaste for Saddam Hussein, as he ended up as a political enemy of the United States. But in our prior history, men with the name *Hussein* from the Middle East were actually held in good diplomacy and in high regard. King Hussein of Jordan was a political ally of Middle East peace and the Western world. Then there is King Hussein of Egypt, who was not as friendly toward the States but not considered to be hostile against the United States or the West.

The origin of the name *Obama* is not quite as identifiable.[66] It appears to have been *Osama* in Kenya, and it may refer to *bending, or leaning*. It may also mean *willing to consider another perspective, compromising*. The name *Osama* is Arabic, and it references *a female lion*, or to be *lionlike*.[67] *Usama* is a reference for a lion, in general,

---

64 *Baracks and Obamas Born in Kenya* (n.d.): n. pag. *Baracks and Obamas Born in Kenya*. Breaking News English, 08 Nov. 2008. Web. 13 Jan. 2014. http://www.breakingnewsenglish.com/0811/081108-names.html.

65 *Quranic Names*. Quran Club, n.d. Web. 13 Jan. 2014. http://quranicnames.com/hussein/.

66 *Wiki Names*. N.p., 05 Nov. 2008. Web. 13 Jan. 2014. http://wiki.name.com/en/ Obama History and Origin.

67 *BabyNames.com*, N.p., Web. 13, Jan. 2014. http://www.babynames.com/name/Osama.

especially a male lion. Just by name alone, it actually points to the likes of a leader who is able to listen to both sides and different perspectives. Does a name automatically match everybody's personality? Surely not. But is it ironic to have such a name, born in the month of Leo, the lion? One of the things in referencing Barack's destiny versus happenstance is how things like this keep building a case for those who are meant to be, or who are, religiously speaking … *ordained.*

I stated in the last chapter that there was something special about our sixteenth president, Abraham Lincoln, in conjunction with President John F. Kennedy (JFK), which I believe set a precedent toward the future of the US presidency. In a speculative but warranted observation, there is what Michael Barone calls a "sixteen-year itch" in American politics, as it relates to an election year.[68] It has been observed since the election of JFK in 1960, when a candidate rises up with a relatively short amount of political experience, the country is willing to chance youthful experience versus that of a more-seasoned candidate. This favored the Democratic Party in this case. After Kennedy, in 1976 the country chose a peanut farmer, one-term governor of Georgia, as its president—a man named Jimmy Carter. Then in 1992, the nation elected William Jefferson Clinton, a forty-six-year-old Arkansas governor who arguably would not have won without the interference of Texas billionaire H. Ross Perot as a third-party candidate, which took away some key conservative votes from the incumbent Republican president, George H. W. Bush. Then, of course, the 2008 outcome favored President Obama.

What are we looking at? Along with this political itch theory, we see something mystical. Obama just happens to be the fourth person chosen in this political theory of a sixteen-year itch. We are reminded that 16 is 4 x 4. Abraham Lincoln was the sixteenth president, and he had to manage and lead a country through the Civil War in regard to the nation's survival and slavery issues. John Fitzgerald Kennedy

---

[68]   Barone, Michael. "The 16-year Itch." *The Wall Street Journal* (n.d.): n. pag. *American Enterprise Institute for Public Policy Research.* 08 Jan. 2008. Web. 13 Jan. 2014. http://www.aei.org/article/politics-and-public-opinion/elections/the-16-year-itch-article/.

has coinciding implications with the president who preceded him by one hundred years, as our thirty-fifth president (3 +5 = 8).

Then you have Barack Obama from Illinois, who becomes the forty-fourth president, and he duplicates some of the historical moments of Abraham Lincoln, including a train ride before his inauguration and using the same Bible used by Lincoln for his swearing-in ceremony. The number 4 again is the number of universal values and significance. More than any other candidate in the primary process of 2008, Barack represented a universal presence of appeal. One of his main campaign issues was universal health care, also a passion of the late Senator Ted Kennedy as well as the Clintons. The concern was that there were approximately forty-four million US people who had no medical coverage at the time. Again, we are looking at 44, or a double 4. So the worldly effects are multiplied beyond the norm. More than just the attentions as a national figure, Barack seemed to have universal appeal, at least at the time before the 2008 presidential election.

In September 2008, the BBC had taken a poll of the international response, and in seventeen of the twenty-two survey nations, it was indicated that most expected relations with the rest of the world would improve if Obama were to be elected instead of his counterpart, Republican Senator John McCain.[69] Another poll made by *Reader's Digest* responded overwhelmingly in the same manner, including countries like Britain, Spain, Mexico, Finland, Spain, Sweden, and Indonesia. Russia scored the lowest, although their results still had Obama edging out McCain. The Australians and New Zealanders felt strongly about the matter of opinion, along with Germany, Italy, France, and the Netherlands.[70]

For instance, when Obama visited abroad in July 2008, a crowd of nearly two hundred thousand showed up in Berlin's Victory Column

[69] "All Countries in BBC Poll Prefer Obama over McCain." *BBC World Service Press Ofice.* BBC, 09 Oct. 2008. Web. 13 Jan. 2014. http://www.bbc.co.uk/pressoffice/pressreleases/stories/2008/09_september/10/poll.shtm

[70] Lam, Andrew. "Obamamania Conquers the World." New America Media, 22 Oct. 2008. Web. 13 Jan. 2014. http://news.newamericamedia.org/news/view_article.html?article_id=e9769290b21598b0191bb18ae57d5a24

to hear the man. At times along the US campaign trails, people fainted in the crowd as they enthusiastically welcomed him and wanted to hear from the well-spoken presidential contender.

A bestselling book in Germany by Christoph von Marscall in 2007, entitled *Barack Obama—Der schwarze Kennedy*, also undergirded the excitement as it made comparisons to the dearly beloved JFK, who encouraged the teardown of the Berlin Wall, in light of the struggles between the Communist support of East Germany versus the more democratic West Germany.[71] Along with his disagreement from the beginning of the war in Iraq, Obama spoke of ending the war, with the reduction of American troop occupation beginning in 2010. The media coverage was accused of biased coverage, compared to the treatment and media time for Senator McCain's campaign.

Now let us go beyond the personality and the charisma of the man who outshined his opponents at that particular time of running for the Democratic presidential nomination. We can easily say that Oprah Winfrey's 2007 endorsement put the strongest winds under the Obama candidacy, enormously sparking him as a leading contender, as she was voted time and again to be one of the most influential woman in the world in the first decade of the twenty-first century.[72] Her endorsement might have made the difference in the Democratic nomination, as stated by some political pundits.

We could also entertain how the Kennedy family, led by the late senior statesmen, Senator Edward Kennedy of Massachusetts, was the greatest momentum shift to skyrocket the young senator from Illinois, as they chose to support Obama in January 2008 as the Democratic candidate[73]. We could even surmise that if the election had another

[71] Von Marscall, 2007.

[72] "Oprah Winfrey's Endorsement of Barack Obama." *Wikipedia, the Free Encyclopedia*. N.p., 25 Nov. 2013- modified. Web. 13 Jan. 2014. http://en.wikipedia.org/wiki/Oprah_Winfrey's_endorsement_of_Barack_Obama

[73] Milligan, Susan, ed. "Ted Kennedy Endorsing Obama." Editorial. *Boston Globe* [Boston, MA] 27 Jan. 2008: n. p. http://www.boston.com/news/politics/politicalintelligence/2008/01/ted_kennedy_end.html

two or three months, Hillary would have steamed-rolled pass Barack to regain the position of the Democratic front-runner; therefore, placing her in position to have been the first woman president in the history of the United States of America.

I believe there were universal effects, both seen and unseen, that was involved in this presidential destiny. Each person or group was a tool of purpose and distinction, though not necessarily the answer to how or why.

I surmise that Obama's election was the result of the seed planted by the efforts of his forerunners of civil justice and the tally of civilian suffering too great to bear. I believe President Obama was the recipient of a numerically based seed principle sown, into the soil of this great country by the efforts of the Civil Rights Movement of the '50s and '60s. His election was the harvest, but the sacrifices of bravery and courage of its leader, Dr. Martin Luther King Jr., coupled with the bloodshed of many others, such as Medgar Evers and the three young civil rights leaders depicted in the movie, *Mississippi Burning*, was the beginning of what eventually came forth in the fall of 2008. This consecration seed of sacrifice is stated by many African American leaders in their fields today, including Oprah Winfrey.[74] Let's consider how this powerful seed was planted and comes in line with the time I am now revealing, as it relates to the seasons of Joseph.

> Truly, truly, I say to you, unless a grain of wheat falls into the Earth and dies, it remains alone; but if it dies, it bears much fruit. (John 12:24 NASB)

> I tell you the truth, unless a kernel of wheat is planted in the soil and dies, it remains alone. But its death will produce many new kernels—a plentiful harvest of new lives. (John 12:24 NLT)

---

[74] Clifford, Megan. *How Oprah Has Changed the Way We Live.* N.d. CNN, 20 May 2011. Web. 15 Jan. 2014. http://www.cnn.com/2011/SHOWBIZ/TV/05/13/oprah.influence/.

This verse of Scripture sets the pace for understanding the Joseph Principle as a seed principle. Joseph's life was cross-sectioned, broken down, and distributed to and through the dealings of humanity by divine permission, just as Jesus of Nazareth made reference to His own life and the lives of all those who will make the sacrifice to bring forth the best possibilities for others. In the same way a seed is dropped into the ground and transforms into another identity for the intended purpose of bearing fruit for the benefit of its recipients.

Notice how Jesus makes the all-important statement, "Truly, truly," or "Verily, verily," in the New American Standard as well as the King James Versions of the Bible. Anytime this occurs, more than just the poetic harmony it creates, the Master Rabbi is making a double reference to the importance of what He is saying. What makes this truth such a standout is that Jesus of Nazareth was speaking in the same spiritual experience of Joseph. The double emphasis ignites the moment as a high priority of life and its foundations. When Joseph had the double dream, his life changed forever. When Pharaoh's servants each had dreams the same night at about the same time, a verdict was at hand. When the pharaoh had the two dreams, he moved with jet speed to find out what was going on. If the dream stood alone, or was never told or emphasized, it might have been bypassed, and those for whom it was intended as an omen or warning would not have taken the special direction that was needed.

The struggle of the Civil Rights Movement exposed the constant hatred and hypocrisy of the dominant race and culture against its own Constitution and Bill of Rights, which all leaders of states and local government officials swore *upon the Holy Bible* to uphold. The Creator of the holy writ saw it all. Many lives were lost, from the broadcasted to those whose fate was met with silence, and these seeds of sacrifice were spread abroad. So it was in most parts of the United States, but especially down South, as blacks fought for their civil rights while suffering the likes of injustice of the courts on every side. The deadly disease of hatred, envy, and foolish pride infiltrated even police forces who swore to protect all citizens, regardless of color.

The unit of terrorism against any black progression was the Ku Klux Klan, or KKK movement.

One eventful day progressively moved the conscience of men to take the civil rights issue to a higher level of concern and need. That was the bombing of the Sixteenth Street Baptist Church in Birmingham, Alabama.

Even more convincing is *the principle* of the seed planted. "Unless a grain of wheat falls into the earth and dies, it remains alone; but if it dies, it bears much fruit" (John 12:24 RSV). This is a biblical principle, and these words of Jesus cannot be denied. The seed comes into its fruitful development by transformation—opening up to release new life or development of another growth stage. This fruit of evolutionary development that occurs before the actual fruit forms is always greater than the seed itself.

Galatians 6:7 also references the growth of a seed, stating, "For whatsoever a man soweth, that shall he also reap" (KJV). Simply put, *we get back what we plant.* This goes beyond the natural laws of nature; this is a spiritual principle.

Even as we speak of the meteoric rise of President Obama, there were things that took place to bring forth fruit from the bloodshed, the sacrifices, and the natural cycle of a planted seed have to be considered and multiplied. Even if no one in this country wanted to recognize what was happening, I guarantee you this: the Lord God of the heavens saw it all, added it up, and then multiplied and divided to bring forth what He would allow in His predestined future.

Much sacrifice took place before this prophecy was fulfilled. A seed had to be planted before growth of our entire country could occur. Allow me to share some key facts with you from that historic time, which underscores how flammable the situation had become in the South. This, I believe, was the fuse that lit the bomb that exploded the growth in our country that allowed our nation's destiny to be fulfilled.

Many innocent lives were taken during the course of slavery and the Jim Crow laws in the South. Rising Negro organizations, such as the NAACP, the Southern Christian Leadership Conference, and the National Urban League, lit the fire that blazed on September 15, 1963, in Birmingham, Alabama, when during religious services, a bombing took place that shook even the hardest of hearts in the struggle for African American civil rights.

That morning at 10:22 a.m., a sudden explosion occurred between church services at the Sixteenth Street Baptist Church in Birmingham. At the time, twenty-six children were in transition into the basement, right before the sermon was to be given. Four young ladies died, and twenty-two children were injured. The explosion blew a hole in the front wall, destroyed the staircase, but left the lone sanctuary window depicting Jesus knocking on the door. The figure of Jesus was missing a face because of the damage.

The four young ladies were Carol Denise McNair, age eleven; Addie Mae Collins, age fourteen; Cynthia Diane Morris, age fourteen; and Carole Rosamond Robertson, also age fourteen. To add to the grief-stricken community, violence broke out in the city on that very same day, where two other black youngsters lost their lives. Johnny Robinson, age sixteen, was killed by police for throwing rocks at cars driven by whites, and thirteen-year-old Virgil Ware was shot by two white teenagers while he and his brother were riding on a bike.

What needs to be understood at this point is that all innocent blood shed takes high precedence in Scriptures, as injustice that demands judgment. Not excluding all those blacks and whites, Native Americans, etc. over the decades that died because of injustice, but it takes on another level when children are killed in the house of worship! Jesus stated in reference to children, and people harming them – spiritually, emotionally, or physically in any way – is standing on dangerous ground.

> Take heed that you do not despise one of these little ones, for I say to you that in heaven their angels always see the face of My Father who is in heaven. (Matt. 18:10, NJKV)

The funeral services were attended by over eight thousand mourners and about eight hundred clergymen, from across racial and denominational backgrounds, including many whites. Dr. Martin Luther King Jr. was the keynote eulogist, and he condemned the cowardly act, yet resolved that justice would prevail.[75] The bombing galvanized people like never before, and support for human justice finally grew higher than the walls of hate and destruction, mounted against the movement for racial equality.

Birmingham, AL; September 17, 1963. Birmingham riots following church bombing. Damage to the 16th Street Baptist Church, from bombing on September 15, 1963, that killed four black children from the congregation. Church seen through windshield of bomb-damaged car parked nearby. © 1976 MattHerron / Take Stock / The Image Works

---

[75] King, Rev. Dr. Martin Luther, Jr. "Eulogy for the Four Girls Who Were Murdered in the Church in Birmingham." *Sixteenth Street Baptist Church Bombing, Birmingham, AL, 1963.* The King Center, n.d. Web. 15 Jan. 2014. http://www.thekingcenter.org/archive/theme/17841.

ETKS1810930   Birmingham, AL; September 18, 1963. Birmingham funeral for 4 girls killed in Klan church bombing. Martin Luther King speaking at funeral for Carol Denise McNair, Addie Mae Collins, Cynthia Diane Wesley, killed in church bombing. A mourner has collapsed during service, is attended by nurses. Sixth Ave Baptist Church. King said: 'At times life is hard, as hard as crucible steel.' 8,000 attended funeral. © 1976 Matt Herron/Take Stock / The Image Works   NOTE: The copyright notice must include "The Image Works" DO NOT SHORTEN THE NAME OF THE COMPANY
© 1976 Matt Herron/Take Stock / The Image Works

Birmingham, AL; September 18, 1963. Birmingham funeral for 4 girls killed in Klan church bombing. Martin Luther King speaking at funeral for Carol Denise McNair, Addie Mae Collins, and Cynthia Diane Morris, killed in church bombing. A mourner has collapsed during service, is attended by nurses. Sixteenth Baptist Church King said: 'At times life is hard, as hard as crucible steel.' 8,000 attended the funeral. © 1976 MattHerron / Take Stock / The Image Works

A march on Washington, DC, occurred a week later, led by the Congress of Racial Equality (CORE), in revoking memory of the Birmingham bombing and like travesties. Banners declaring, "No More Birminghams" were carried by demonstrators.

On July 2, 1964, President Lyndon B. Johnson signed the Civil Rights Act of 1964, affirming that African Americans should be granted the same rights under the law as the Caucasian citizenship of this nation.

Justice prevailed when four white men representing the United Klans of America were charged and convicted of the heinous crimes. Those men were Robert Chambliss, Thomas Blanton, Herman Frank Cash, and Bobby Frank Cherry. They had used twenty-two sticks of dynamite in the bombing of the church.

Let's examine the seed of sacrifice that was made and how it brought forth fruitfulness, according to the Joseph Principle we have been addressing. Let's examine the carnage, even though it is still hard for me—and likely you—to accept that this actually happened and that people suffered this kind of pain during this stage of American life. When we examine this horrible time, we will see reference to the destiny that Barack Obama is now living out that goes beyond words.

- Twenty-six children were in a procession to lead a youth presentation in church that morning.
- Four young ladies were killed in the blast that took place at the Sixteenth Street Baptist Church.
- Four men—KKK members—committed and were convicted for their heinous crime.
- There were twenty-two sticks of dynamite used in the fatal blast.
- There were twenty-two people injured in the blast.
- About eight thousand mourners attended the service.
- About eight hundred clergymen attended from various Christian denominations and religions.
- The same day, a sixteen-year-old teenager was also shot and killed.
- A little later that afternoon, a thirteen-year-old was also killed.[76]

When we understand and apply gematria to this scenario, we see clearly, the number 4 sticking out like a sore thumb, but the number 4 does not stand alone. The number 11 also comes into the scene as witness to the planting of a sacrificial seed for a future redemption.

Whether you consider the number 22 as separate digits (2 + 2 = 4), add the young girls who were killed, or take a look at those who were convicted of the crime, you see the number 4. Now, if you add the sticks of dynamite to the number of the injured, you now have 44! You

---

[76] "16th Street Baptist Church Bombing." *Wikipedia*. Wikimedia Foundation, 15 Jan. 2014. Web. 15 Jan. 2014. http://en.wikipedia.org/wiki/16th_Street_Baptist_Church_bombing.

have multiple sets of 4, by both gematria and simple facts, and you get 44 by adding up the sticks of dynamite with the injured (22 + 22 = 44).

What time did the blast strike the heart of America at the Sixteenth Street Baptist Church? The blast occurred at 10:22 a.m. Even the time that the explosives went off is crucial to this gematria equation: twenty-two minutes after 10:00 a.m. But an unseen gematria may also be observed. Another way of saying the time of 10:22 a.m. is thirty-eight minutes before the eleventh hour, or (3 + 8 =11).

Just like the traumatic betrayal of Joseph by his brothers' unthinkable evil plot, we see that Heaven was already mapping out a redemptive plan against pure evil. The number of children to be involved with the youth presentation on that day was twenty-six, with a gematria of 8 (2 + 6 = 8). Yes, the number of a new beginning, and oh my God, was a new beginning getting ready to begin!

We see a serious pattern that goes beyond the natural order of things. There were not three or five or two or six young people or church members killed. The KKK members intended to kill many more in that blast, but four were killed. Three of the young ladies were fourteen years old. One—only one—was eleven years old. Four young, beautiful children, all girls, were killed, and *one* was eleven years old—the youngest one (4 x 11 = 44). Is that stretching it? Okay, the numerical summation of the four little angels by their combined ages is fifty-three years (5 + 3 = 8)! Again, the name *Joseph* means "to add, add up, or on." Let's continue to see how the Joseph Principle explodes in this scenario.

The location of the blast was the *Sixteenth Street* Baptist Church (16 = 4 x 4). Sixteenth Street Baptist Church is located on the corner of Sixteenth Street and Sixth Avenue, in Birmingham. Note that 16 + 6 – 22! Integral reduced value? Two plus 2 equal 4. Come on now!

This crime propelled action on a national level, which was another black-eyed event in American politics and civil unrest that was broadcast around the world. This horrific event occurred only two and a half months before President John F. Kennedy was assassinated. It should have been JFK who signed and legislated the bill in Washington, DC, but instead, it was President Lyndon B.

Johnson who signed the Civil Rights Bill of 1964 on June 30.[77] The act was passed by the eighty-eighth US Congress. Which congressional sitting was it? The *eighty-eighth!* We see that 88 is two 44s (44 + 44 = 88)! All this was—and is—more, so much more than a national and international phenomenon of grief and sadness. The planting of the Joseph Principle is unlike anything I have ever witnessed as a researcher. As indicated earlier in chapter 8, without a doubt, the Almighty saw it, declared it, prepared it, and searched it out, in determining the ultimate sacrificial seed that was sown, its cost, and total impact on the entire world (Job 28:27).

The Renewed Sanctuary of the 16th Street Baptist Church

As a historical landmark of the Civil Rights Movement, this is presently the beautiful edifice of the Sixteenth Street Baptist Church of Birmingham, AL, where the bombing took place over 50 years ago. In remembrance of the four little angels, their families, and all that took place on that fateful day, thousands visit the Milestone exhibition gallery annually in the Birmingham Civil Rights Institute, connected to the church.
Photo Credit, Karen Dawkins,©FamilyTravelsonaBudget.com; 2014.

---

[77] 1964 Civil Rights Act. (2014, February 05). *Wikipedia.* Retrieved February 05, 2014, from http://en.wikipedia.org/wiki/1964_Civil_Rights_Act.

Importantly—and as many of you have already observed and figured out—we see that exactly forty-four years later Barack Obama was elected as our nation's first African American president. His election, without a doubt, was divinely orchestrated and ordained, but not without the fearsome price of bloodshed and martyrdom. To be quite honest, the number 4 was both numerically and historically so strong in reference to this information about Barack Obama and his election that I knew when the winds of adversity blew on his reelection campaign for 2012, he would still win. See, he was not only elected forty-four years after the Civil Rights Bill was signed; but also after death of a spiritual martyr, the accepted point man and voice of the movement, Dr. Martin Luther King Jr.

Dr. Martin Luther King Jr. and his colleagues stood by as President Lyndon Baines Johnson signed the Civil Rights Bill. Only four years later, Dr. King was assassinated for the cause he so triumphantly stood for. The magnitude of King's life and death has far-reaching effects, from earth to glory. While researching facts, I was reminded that King was shot and killed in April 1968. I said to myself, *there it is again!* Forty-four years from MLK's death was the year 2012! And 44, now in hindsight, The Lord was showing me four years plus four more years for President Obama. Four years to start his administration and four years to finish, one term of being greater than the other. I will surely leave that up to debate. But even speaking of the Joseph Principle as a time indicator, I thought about how ironic it was that Obama was the first African American president running as an incumbent and his Republican opponent in 2012 was Mitt Romney, the first Mormon to run for the US presidency. So what does that have to do with this revelation? The founder of the Mormon faith was *Joseph* Smith!

The awesome theme of the life of Joseph from Egypt was that heaven gave him a dream, layered in other dreams, and his life and the difficult circumstances of that life made him the outstanding person he was. When we consider how Dr. Martin Luther King Jr. is now memorialized on the Washington Mall, in the District of Colombia, after giving the visionary "I Have a Dream" speech,[78] we must at least begin to see and look upward concerning the events of these men and where they are leading us today. Without apology, I am delivering the message to you that I know and believe that God is trying to tell us something—*right now*—regarding the season in which we are now living and what is required of us as we move forward. How in the world does a civil rights leader receive an honor that is reserved only for presidents? Dr. Martin Luther King Jr.'s memorial is located on the National Mall in the vicinity of the Lincoln Memorial!

Dr. King's famous speech was themed in the biblical principles of faith, hope, and love, which are also themed in the US Constitution, the Preamble, and other early documents on which our country was founded: faith in God, hope for a greater day, love for God and mankind. Even so, many evangelists of the past, from north to south, held prejudices and outright racism in their hearts, under the guise of religion. Dr. Martin Luther King Jr. was more of a social-gospel preacher than an evangelical preacher. Yet he compellingly made a pitch to save the souls of the evangelical preachers and their associated congregations from their hatred, which was going to damn them before the throne of the Most High. One of the old sayings in predominantly black churches was, "Everybody talkin' about heaven ain't goin' there."

Dr. King saved many souls from their hypocrisy and helped us all to look deep within ourselves to see if the true love of God was really abiding in our hearts. His motto and platform of nonviolence demonstrated over and over the fruit of tough, implanted love. The Bible teaches that, without true love, the true God is not your real Father (1 John 4:20). Don't get me wrong. I am writing about the hypocrisy of general religious conservative masses who say what seems to be true, but the motives of the heart are nothing short of sour grapes and wicked hors d'oeuvres.

---

[78] News, ABC. "Martin Luther King's Speech: 'I Have a Dream' - The Full Text." *ABC News.* ABC News Network, n.d. Web. 13 Jan. 2014. http://abcnews.go.com/ Politics/martin-luther-kings-speech-dream-full-text/story?id=14358231.

Destiny is not just the occurrence of good, but it is the acceptance of the bitter, along with the sweet. Just as we would rather only talk about life, we must sometimes face the aroma of death. Just as we want to speak about our favorite team making the World Series or the Super Bowl, somebody's team has to lose. And just like we want to think everyone is going up yonder to the pie in the sky, we need to face the truth that the book that speaks about heaven is also the book that gives warning against a terrible place called hell. When we speak about destiny, or what is meant to be, we are referencing what the Almighty already knows ahead of time, though we still have to live through it as humanity. Destiny is sometimes tragic and unmerciful. The Bible speaks about the eventual judgment of the wicked—not just eternal damnation but horrible earthly suffering from things that are set for and formalized in evil.

CHAPTER 12

A BLUE MOON REVELATION

I already know and anticipate many varying opinions on this dissertation intended to reveal the Lord God's goodness, to unfold and unlock keys of understanding. Some may accuse me of being New Age or of walking in the path of satanic rituals, as if the Evil One is the originator of time and space. But I am at peace with sharing this message that has been revealed to me, and my domestic and church families know better than to believe I would deliver anything other than God's truth as He reveals it to me. For me to speak something and have it come to pass is nothing new to them. I am grateful to my heavenly Father for being so patient with me and allowing me to write, to endure my trials and tribulations over the eight years of coming in line with this progressive awareness.

Quite honestly, He has been working on me since I was a child, as touched on in the opening chapter of this work. I know deep down that I am not worthy to deliver such a message, except for the grace and mercy He has provided. And yes, the price of being a recipient of this grace and responsibility is hard to describe. I know and believe that the one who spoke to my heart and mind so clearly that day in my closet as a young teenager also knew that allowing my mother to pass away at the tender age of forty-four, leaving her loved ones behind, would bring about a full-circle revelation—the Joseph Principle, the

44 factor. My favorite legend of a football player is Coatesville Senior High School's Abel Joe, who wore the number 44, and so did I, as a junior and senior high school football player—yet it still did not register as a memorial to my mother, Hattie Viola Merchant Hunt.

Can the Almighty direct our steps and download knowledge ahead of time? I wanted to wear the number 44, after my high school football idol, Abel Joe of the famous Joe family in our city, which includes the 1965 NFL's rookie of the year and former NCAA football coach, Billy Joe. At the time, I did not equate my mother's death, with the number. Ironically, even though Abel graduated seven years before me, we not only lived in the same neighborhood, our mothers died within three weeks of each other. Abel had held the school record for the most yards gained in a single season, in a career, and touchdowns scored as a running back. I broke his single season rushing record in my senior year, as a fullback. What was also unusual is that I had to wear the #42 my sophomore year, before wearing #44 my last two years. Jesus of Nazareth was the 42nd generation from Abraham by genealogy, and I am persuaded within the seasons of Joseph, he will represent the Messiah as the 44th generation as written.

It's not easy to step away from what one repeatedly has been exposed to as traditional truth, but God must stretch us for us to overcome the past and to introduce us to the present dilemmas we are now facing. That's the value of learning the Spirit of the law rather than just learning the black and white of the written law.

When I was sharing just a portion of this knowledge in a seminar the fall of 2008 on the Saturday before the general election, I will never forget when a precious elderly fellow parishioner of the church, where the seminar was held, communicated with me. I asked for opinions concerning the material I had just presented called, "The Seasons of Joseph," and he stated (in paraphrase), "You [meaning me, the author] cannot be right in sharing this information with the church, because Obama supports abortion, and I cannot conscientiously vote for him in the upcoming election."

I had already shared that the truth has to support itself and that I was not there endorsing any candidate, one over the other. Yes, I stated that I was persuaded that Obama would win the presidency because of the patterns to which I was made privy. I don't necessarily believe that this white gentleman thought I was there to endorse President Obama only because I was a fellow African American. However, as I was writing chapter 11 of this book, it crossed my mind many times that there would be readers who might think I was saying President Barack Obama is a God-fearing man and a fully committed Christian, worthy of the support of all Christian masses. I am not saying that; but I am saying he was presdestined to be elected.

I know one thing: he is a great man who came from a different perspective of moral ethics that I hold dear. I respect him and his family dearly, and I pray for them that they may walk into a greater destiny of revealing truth. You see, prophetic spokesmen like myself are called to speak and expound on what has been revealed to them, in spite of what the masses believe. Christians, including myself, need to read and reread the Bible and discover freshness in the Ancient of Days and be open to the Spiritual Guide, the Holy Spirit. But no,

I am not always on target and correct in everything I say and do. Perfection is who I serve, *not* who I am, but I am striving.

In the first week of September 2008, prior to the presidential election, I declared at the Holy Trinity Church of God in Christ (renamed The A. D. Baxter Memorial COGIC) in Coatesville, Pennsylvania, that Barack Obama was going to be president, and Senator Hillary Clinton was going to be a part of his administration and his extension in the world. This declaration was not based upon my political biases and persuasions. Instead, this revelation was given to me by the Spirit of God, and He didn't care whether I approved or disapproved of the man or woman who might be elected, if that was the case. I was merely sharing with the congregation what the Lord had shared and confirmed with me *seven months prior to that moment.*

In sharing the Joseph Principle, I am sharing that the Lord God has placed signs in the earth, and through prophets and scribes, to record the history of Israel and the nations of the world of its day. It's a shame that some theologians believe the writings were nothing more than fables and tales only worthy of allegorical examples for human morality. No, His Word is His very breath to assure life and grant prosperity to those who uphold its truth and guidelines.

Jeffery Grant strived to communicate in his book, *The Signature of God,* that God used the Bible codes to self-address the letter and the messages He was trying to convey.[79] This text piggybacked off what Michael Drosin wrote in *The Bible Code,* which was so compelling.[80] I believe that the Creator has allowed me also to tap into one of his echoing streams of liquid love sent to the human race, to allow us to know His reality. Yes, just like the Great Shepherd's window that was divinely spared in the aftermath of the Sixteenth Street Baptist Church of Birmingham, Alabama; though the face of Jesus

---

[79] Grant, 1999.
[80] Drosin, 1998.

was broken out by the blast.[81] You can almost hear His echoes some fifty years later, as if to say, "I stood and am still standing to knock on the hearts of men, to provide them with the Shepherd's care that they so desperately need." I can hear the heart of the Jesus sharing, "My face is hidden through the deliberate hatred of men's hearts, but My hands are still extended, to whosoever will." (Rev. 22:17).

Joseph was more than gifted to do what he did, but he was a conduit the Lord God planted among us to guarantee the future of His re-visitation through the coming Messiah, an ever-present spiritual enablement providing love for all in the present. As stated through Jacob and Moses, these blessings are perpetual and will last until the kingdom comes ... literally (Matt. 6:9–10). His exemplary life, just like the seed principle of Jesus of Nazareth as we discussed in chapter 11, is bearing fruit and will continue to do so in whosoever takes the message of this great news to heart.

This book is entitled *44°* in celebration of another unique way that the Benevolent Creator chose to unveil His redemptive plan of the ages, in synchronization with the heavens and earth. He waited for such a time as this to further demonstrate His prevailing promises to Joseph, using the sun, moon, and stars as witnesses, as it relates to His promise of a coming Messiah. Consider the following statement concerning this phenomenon:

> The seasons are caused by the non-perpendicular rotation of the Earth's axis to its orbital plane (the flat plane made through the center of mass (barycenter) of the solar system (near or within the Sun) and the successive locations of Earth during the year. This currently makes an angle of about 23.44° (called the "obliquity of the ecliptic"); while the axis keeps its orientation with respect to inertial space.

---

[81] "16th Street Baptist Church Bombing." *Wikipedia.* Wikimedia Foundation, 15 Jan. 2014. Web. 15 Jan. 2014. <http://en.wikipedia.org/wiki/16th_Street_Baptist_Church_bombing>.

As a consequence, for half the year (from around 20 March to 22 September) the northern hemisphere is inclined toward the Sun, with the maximum around 21 June, while for the other half year the southern hemisphere has this distinction, with the maximum around 21 December. The two moments when the inclination of the Earth's rotational axis has maximum effect are called the solstices.

At the northern solstice the subsolar point reaches to 23.44° north, known as the Tropic of Cancer. Likewise, at the southern solstice the same thing happens for latitude 23.44° south, known as the Tropic of Capricorn. The sub-solar point will cross every latitude between these two extremes exactly twice per year.[82]

In my layman's terms, the earth is always at a precise angle to the sun as it spins on its axis. The earth travels around the sun, and the projection of the sun's rays affects the amount of sunlight we receive and the length of time it appears during a day or night. The maximum and the minimum points of contact cause the sun to be farther away from the earth or closer in proximity. These extreme points, June 21 and December 21, are the beginning of the summer season and the beginning of the winter season. We understand that the summer solstice produces the longest day and the shortest night, and December 21 begins wintertime, with the longest night and the shortest day.

While the Earth remains, seedtime and harvest, cold and heat, summer and winter, day and night, shall not cease. (Gen. 8:22 ESV)

---

[82] "Solstice." *Wikipedia*. Wikimedia Foundation, updated 09 Jan. 2014. Web. 15 Jan. 2014. http://en.wikipedia.org/wiki/Solstice

Notice that the text specifically refers to the highest and lowest points of the earth's relationship to the sun. Spring and fall are not specifically mentioned but are alluded to as "seedtime and harvest." Once again, we see the coupling of four distinct groups, along with a world that will remain in its present state until the Messiah comes.

When I researched and found not only projected seasons for a year but exact dates and exact times of each occurrence, I was exhilarated! The synchronization and harmony of the planets blows me away! I am amazed at its wonder, and as I shared, I am not even a science buff. But with my naked eye, through studying the knowledge of others, I see the handiwork of God, fulfilling the messages that He is the only ultimate sovereign power who organized this unfathomable universe. He has a special love relationship with the earth and with the eternal beings that walk in human shells called *bodies* or *temples*.

> The heavens proclaim the glory of God. The skies display his craftsmanship. Day after day they continue to speak; night after night they make him known. They speak without a sound or word; their voice is never heard. Yet their message has gone throughout the Earth, and their words to all the world. God has made a home in the heavens for the sun. It bursts forth like a radiant bridegroom after his wedding. It rejoices like a great athlete eager to run the race. The sun rises at one end of the heavens and follows its course to the other end. Nothing can hide from its heat. (Ps. 19:1–6 NLT)

So, in reference to this wonder of our solar system and the earth's relationship with the sun and the moon, the title *44°* seemed fitting for this message. Hopefully this study has helped us to change some of our notions and ideas by looking, reading, and researching, and we can continue to listen to God's messages and learn, thus live in a greater destiny and season because of this unveiling truth. We can now come out of the snowy winter into the brilliance of spring!

The Almighty chose Joseph to display His might and wisdom in the earth. He was chosen for God's ultimate grace and intentions to be displayed in a fallen world of humanity. Does the Creator forget what He has promised? Never! As already stated, He never does anything in the earth without communicating in increments to his chosen vessels on earth. Two of those chosen vessels, as we have seen with affirming truth, were Jacob (whose name was changed to *Israel*) and Moses. I trust their preserved words, and so be it.

The gospel of John says, "For the law was given by Moses, but grace and truth came by Jesus Christ" (John 1:17 KJV). So true! All ultimate grace and truth comes from the Messiah, who I believe was Jesus of Nazareth, in His first earthly assignment. Joseph of Egypt was absolutely that one who God's ultimate grace was displayed. The law was sanctioned and given to Moses, the Lawgiver, but ultimately, the law *was given* to him; he did not initiate it. So when we are blessed, we can always look to the hills and remember—to the fourth power— His faithfulness! Abraham, Isaac, Jacob, and Joseph are four men in descending order. Jesus came and fulfilled the sufferings of what He initially gave Joseph before his earthly arrival.

The book of Revelation, the last book of the New Testament, includes a powerful reference:

> And after these things I saw four angels standing on the four corners of the Earth, holding the four winds of the Earth, that the wind should not blow on the Earth, nor on the sea, nor on any tree. (Rev. 7:1 KJV)

Upon first reading the phrase, "four corners of the Earth" may seem confusing because the earth is round, and circles or spheres do not have corners. However, we can recognize through science that we have a north, south, east, and west, and thus we often refer to "a corner of the globe." So if we accept and understand this, we will see a greater truth. If the sun and moon are spherical shapes, like the earth, then the sun (the greater one) has the greater four corners, and the moon (the lesser one) has four corners. Both spheres manage our days and nights, and thus we experience and see the effects of the greater 4 and the lesser 4 and their companionship with the earth at large. So along with the earth rotating on its axis, we experience the degrees of their effect, both literally and by angles, thus, *44 degrees*.

We see the number 4 as a universal truth and worldly connector, but what about the number 11? Have you heard of solar flares? For whatever strange reason, the sun's energy produces a greater combustion every eleven years! The earth just experienced one recently in March of 2012. This cycle produced the strongest of the flares, as it engaged the eleventh year of its weather cycle. This activity, according to NASA, ended in 2013.[83]

Now, you observant readers and students of faith: did you see the numbers of the high of the summer solstice, as well as the low of the winter solstice? I was waiting for a few paragraphs to underscore the natural but spiritual affirmation of such glorious, inspiring knowledge. The degree 23.44 is broken down by integral reduced value: it is 2 + 3 + 4 + 4 = 13! And once again, the third step that brings it into a single digit is 1 + 3 = 4! These are Anglican measurements, I know, and they seem to be biased. But as stated earlier in chapter 10, the far-reaching extension of Joseph's covenant favor still remained with England and is now more fruitful through the English Channel, and influences the Western world. The Almighty foreknew the time and season of this unique unveiling, and He allowed it to be precise to the world that is now most enjoined by the English language and measurements.

In all that has been shared, I desire everyone to see the hand and mind of the Almighty, who knew of the events, before they took place. The whole universe is connected to not just the Father of glory – The Almighty Creator, but also is embedded by the numerical identity

---

[83] "Sun's 2013 Solar Activity Peak Is Weakest in 100 Years." *Space.com*. Ed. Megan Gannon. N.p., 12 July 2013. Web. 15 Jan. 2014. http://www.space.com/21937-sun-solar-weather-peak-is-weak.html.

of the Messiah. These are the seasons of Joseph that will usher in a greater time; that of the coming Messiah. The election of Barack Obama as the 44th president of the leading nation of the international community was meteoric and a phenomenon as a first, like Joseph's exaltation in Egypt. It serves as a major sign that we cannot afford to be ignored. Globally, something is unfolding that will only get stronger, moving forward. The prophecies will be fulfilled and it's time for all to take heed, unless we choose to ignore it to our own demise. It's a season and this unveiling is an extended forecast of patterns to come. This knowledge is now being unveiled to create a fresh angle of *44°*, to assist willing hearts and minds into an alliance of due reverence for the designer of life. I have much more precision to share, but this present road has to come to an end for now.

In conclusion, we are familiar with the phrase, "Once in a blue moon." On August 20, 2013, I traveled to my father's and mother's graves to honor what would have been my father's eighty-eighth birthday (or so I thought). I knew my book was significant, dedicated to my mother, and I wanted to give my respects accordingly before I finished my collection of information. As I sat in the grass, plucking grass and weeds from the edging around my father's veteran's gravesite plaque, I noticed behind me two ladies and their dog attending another gravesite.

I was locked into my thoughts and memories of both parents and how my mom's death at age forty-four was so significant to what I was about to share with the world, when one of the ladies walked up behind me and offered me flowers to place in the vase. I found out it was a mother and her daughter. It was startling and sweet that these total strangers offered to participate in my precious moments of reflection and recollection.

"Yes, thank you. That is so nice of you," I said. The woman kindly placed the flowers in the vase and used their extra water to nurture the wilting flowers. This woman shared that her husband had passed away after a second round of cancer treatment that proved to be too much. I then told her that my mother passed quickly in like fashion and that I had just lost a good friend in the church that I pastored at about the same time of her husband's death.

This woman did not realize how she blessed me. Her name was Mrs. Hamilton. I had desired to bring flowers to my parents' graves as I usually do, but because of the late hour and the setting sun, I arrived near the cemetery later than usual, so I didn't stop for flowers.

Earlier in the day, I heard on one of the Philadelphia news channels that there would be a blue moon. A blue moon occurs seven times every nineteen years, and therefore, it's a rarity. It is also termed such because when a season of three months has three full moons, the blue moon occurs in a season four times, squeezing two appearances into a thirty-day period. (Notice the number four factored in again.) When a blue moon sequence occurs, that year will have a total of thirteen full moons, instead of the normal twelve.

When the kind woman placed the flowers in my parents' vase, I immediately noticed the two golden yellow blooms that looked like thick daisies. I thought of how they represented my parents. Then as fast as that thought came, I wondered, *How many blooms are there in total? Could it be of further significance?* I counted anxiously, and lo and behold, there were fourteen reddish-pink daffodil blooms. That's sixteen blooms! Yes, a 4 x 4 combination! Double 4s! God is awesome!

If you and me can see Him and believe in His works, we will be blessed. This blessing, for me, was so unique and precise because the three stems of the reddish-pink blooms held stamens for five blooms each, but one set was missing a bloom.

The kind ladies and I said our good-byes, and they left me alone to reflect on the astonishing moment. Before I left the cemetery, I felt compelled to go over to the gravesite the two ladies had visited to see the floral arrangement they had left behind. It was a beautiful, large sunflower in a pot, surrounded by the flowers mentioned above, plus plenty of white blooms from different species of flowers—easily over fifty blooms. I could not help but think that, out of all those blooms, she gave me the sixteen remaining, telling me that, though the flowers were a little wilted, the water would revive them shortly.

I returned again to my parents' gravesite, and sure enough, the blooms had already perked up, signifying to me how my parents were really blessed people. I tell you, a sequence like this could only occur "once in a blue moon"!

Soon thereafter I texted my family about my special evening. Then, our second-oldest daughter reminded me that it was my father's *eighty-ninth* birthday—not his eighty-eighth. I boldly corrected her, stating that was her grandpop's eighty-eighth birthday. I was certain my mom died at forty-four years of age, and my special moment was capped off with the knowledge that my dad's age of eighty-eight at the time of his death doubled the number of her age.

When I later discussed this with my wife, she, too, corrected me. My father would have been age eighty-nine on this day. My blue moon experience was immediately altered! To make matters worse, I'd put my so-called spiritual revelation on family chat. *I was wrong.* Publically so!

While seeking consolation, I wondered how old Joseph was when his life changed forever, when he was separated from and humiliated by his brothers. I remembered that he was seventeen years old. Did that fit into my gematria considerations? So, on this particular date, my father would have been eighty-nine years old, and $8 + 9 = 17$.

The gracious Spirit of the Lord began to speak to my heart:

> I want to show you again and again that what you are dealing with is truly from Me. I had the ladies meet you where you were—out of nowhere, as strangers—with sixteen blooms and water. So it is that as you release this knowledge in the earth, wilting flowers will begin to bloom again. I am showing you the end from the beginning of the season about which you are now writing.

I wanted to shout out in spirit, "How sweet it is!" like Jackie Gleason's catchphrase on the American sitcom *The Honeymooners* six decades ago.[84] I had thought my miscalculation messed up the evaluation, but it was not so! Repeating—a blue moon occurs seven times every nineteen years, and 7 + 1 + 9 = 17! And the final step in integral reduced value is 8, the number of new beginnings. So, my friend and neighbor, *let it be*. It's time to let it be. It's time to be spiritually free, to believe it all. He's real!

May the Lord's grace, like water, continue to refresh our lives, which only bloom for a moment before our natural frame goes back into the dust and eternity meets us face-to-face.

> And many of those who sleep in the dust of the earth shall awake: some to everlasting life and some to shame and everlasting contempt *and* abhorrence. And the teachers *and* those who are wise shall shine like the brightness of the firmament, and those who turn many to righteousness (to uprightness and right standing with God) [shall give forth light] like the stars forever and ever. (Dan. 12:2–3 AMP)

Please don't reserve your eternal destiny to rest in the hands of everlasting regrets and judgment. Do something about it as soon as possible. That is not the love of God or His purpose for you reading this presentation of truth in 44°. It is God's perfect will to see that all creation bows in total submission to His lordship in your life. Just as I have been humbled to be chosen to reveal such, you and I together are called to humble ourselves before Him in everyday life. Please read and meditate on the invitation page to secure the knowledge of the heart that we all so desperately need and actually want. God bless you on this journey of getting to know Him more intimately, from the precise angle of 44°.

---

[84] http://en.wikipedia.org/wiki/The_Honeymooners.

BELIEVE IT OR NOT- LET'S PRAY

During a cold, wintery season, I checked out a DVD from a local library in Chester County. It's actually one of my favorites of old: Albert Finney's *Scrooge, the Musical.* The charge is fairly low unless you go a week over. Well, a week went by, and I knew I would have extra—but not over-the-top—charges. I was determined to return it before the two weeks was up, but things came up again, and now I faced the two-week deadline. Twelve inches of snow fell into our area on the very day I needed to have it back before the next round of higher costs. The DVD sat on my counter, but I kept allowing other things to take priority and did not take action as needed. Therefore, it cost me more.

You don't want to keep putting your eternal soul on hold. In *44°*, we have touched on the value of the number 4 and how it concerns this most important matter of the eternal soul.

Four things are established between God and man on the earth, and they stand out as truth in regards to His love and mercy for you and me.

- **God:** The almighty, benevolent Creator
- **Creation:** What He has created with purpose and design
- **Redemption:** God's answer to man's sinful condition to line up with Him and live eternally in His presence
- **Life:** The fulfillment of purpose and blessing for mankind eternally

Four Universal Principles of Life

1. **Creation**- First points to a Creator and His character.
2. **Instruction**- Connects to His all-encompassing authority and wisdom of life.
3. **Redemption**- Speaks of man's free will and act to rebel but yet his need of salvation.
4. **Life**- Maintains the purpose and standards that preserve the blessings of God's original intent and design.

The Four Spiritual Laws of Eternal Life

1. Admit that you are a sinner, not in reference to others but to God and His holiness (Rom. 3:10, 23).
2. Be willing to turn from your way (repent) to His way, the way your heavenly Father ordained as He has revealed it through the Messiah, Jesus of Nazareth (John 14:6, 10:27; Rom. 6:23).
3. Believe that the Messiah (Christ) did what was required to secure your redemption/atonement by His death, burial, and resurrection (Rom. 10:9–13).
4. Through prayerful commitment, invite Jesus to be your Lord and Messiah for the rest of your life (John 1:12).

Your prayerful commitment might be similar to the following prayer, but God hears and knows your heart:

Dear Heavenly Father:

I acknowledge that I need You in my life. I admit that I was born a sinner with a mind-set to do things my way without Your approval. But now I give myself to You, and I choose to believe in Your way of salvation for my eternal soul. I believe in Jesus as my Lord and Savior, which includes His death, burial, and resurrection. Please come into my heart and change me, to be the kind of person You want me to be—a person who seeks You daily and desires to please You. For Your glory and honor, I give my life to You. Amen.

What if you are not ready for this kind of commitment? What if you are not ready to change or even concede that Jesus is the Messiah at this time?

Here is a follow-up prayer for the future truth and atonement of your soul.

Dear Almighty God and Creator,

I believe that You exist, and I want You to please show me the way of life and salvation. I am unsure about how to relate and commit my life to You in fullness. If Jesus is truly the coming Messiah and Lord, please open my eyes to see and believe as the author has explained. Please teach and show me as I read this book beyond today and consider further what I am reading. Please show me more of your reality in my everyday experience and help me to regain my sincerity of heart. Deliver me from any stubbornness and rebellion that would keep me from believing in You and your truth. Amen.

If you prayed this prayer or have additional questions, please contact us through Trinity United Bible Church in Coatesville, PA where Kevin McCoy Hunt serves as Senior Pastor. We will be happy to pray with and for you, and if you'd like, we can set up time to speak with you by phone or in person. Guiding you to greater is our joy to serve.

Go to www.TUBCfamily.org and complete the *Contact Us* form.

BIBLIOGRAPHY

Bullinger, E. (2005). *Numbers in Scripture*. New York: Cosimo Classics.

Butler, T. (1991) *Holman Bible Dictionary*. Nashville, TN: Holman Bible Publishers.

Drosin, M. (1998). *The Bible Code*. Austin, TX: Touchstone.

Elder, J. (1960). *Prophets, Idols, and Diggers: Scientific Proof of Bible History*. Indianapolis: Bobbs-Merrill.

Fausset, A., Brown, D. & Jamieson, R. (1961). *Jamieson, Fausset & Brown's Commentary on the Whole Bible*. Grand Rapids, MI: Zondervan Pub. House.

Gonzalez, G. & J. Richards. (2004). *The Privileged Planet: How Our Place in the Cosmos Is Designed for Discovery*. Washington, DC: Regnery Publishing.

Grant, J. (1999). *The Signature of God, The Handwriting of God*. NY: Inspirational.

Greison, S. (Director). (2003). *The Search for the Real Mt. Sinai*. [Motion picture]. United States: Exploration Films.

Michalowski, K. (1968). "The Labyrinth Enigma: Archaeology Suggestions." *Journal of Egyptian Archaeology*, Vol.54, 219–22. Egypt Exploration Society.

Rohl, D. (1997). *Pharaohs and Kings: A Biblical Conquest*. NY: Three Rivers Press.

Stone, Jr., P. (2001). *Plucking the Eagle's Wings*. Cleveland, TN: The Voice of Evangelism.

Von Marscall, C. and, von Bieberstein, C. (2007). *Barack Obama: Der schwarze Kennedy*. Orell Füssli.